NO HURRY TO HOREB

Kalu Onwuka

Granada Publishers

Los Angeles, California

No Hurry to Horeb

Copyright ©2014 by Kalu Onwuka

Published in Los Angeles, California by Granada Publishers. Granada Publishers is wholly owned by Granada Publishing Company, Los Angeles, California.

Granada Publishing titles may be purchased in bulk for educational, fundraising or sales promotional use. For more information please e-mail **sales@granadapublishing.com**

All rights reserved. No part of this publication may be reproduced, stored in a retrieval system or transmitted in any form or by any means-electronic, mechanical, digital, photocopy, recording or any other-except for brief quotations in printed reviews, without the written permission of the copyright owner.

Library of Congress Cataloging-in-Publications Data

No Hurry to Horeb/ Kalu Onwuka

LCCN: 2014918589

ISBN: 978-0-9900203-7-0

ISBN: 0990020371

Printed in the United States

DEDICATION

I will like to dedicate this book, *No Hurry to Horeb* which is part of *Ruminations on the Golden Strand* series, to all those who share the gifts of light and love in the world either in formal or informal settings. Yours is not an easy job for Truth is very hard to tell and often falls on deaf ears in a world where the sweet and easy has become the norm. The world may or may not acclaim you but Heaven's promise is never to forget or forsake such as you that labor to keep the gate against the onslaught of darkness.

ACKNOWLEDGMENTS

As always, I will first like to acknowledge Christ Jesus as the Lord of my life. He is my muse and I write through his light. I will like to acknowledge that it is not possible to see through an undertaking such as *Ruminations of the Golden Strand* series without the loyal support of family, friends and well-wishers. You have all been there from the beginning on through to the publication process. I will also like to acknowledge all your assistance for you continue to give me cause to hope for better from humanity. It is such goodness that you show that will help transform the world from what is today to the better that it can be in future.

CONTENTS

Dedication		iii
Acknowledgments		iv
Introduction		vii
Chapter 1	A place on the Mountain	1
Chapter 2	Mustering for the Fight	11
Chapter 3	Winning New Grounds	23
Chapter 4	Call to the Summit	31
Chapter 5	The Noble Fisherman	41
Chapter 6	Light for All	53
Chapter 7	In Greater Measure	63
Chapter 8	Freed by Truth	73
Chapter 9	New Wine for New Vessels	83

CONTENTS

Chapter 10	Vessels set Apart	95
Chapter 11	An Acceptable Threshold	105
Chapter 12	The Keeper is Well-Kept	115
Chapter 13	Place of the Selfless	125
Chapter 14	An Unmistakable Voice	135
Chapter 15	Riches of the Field	143
Chapter 16	The Sweet Spot	153
Chapter 17	Peace that is Priceless	165
Chapter 18	Of Truth, Light and Love	177
Chapter 19	The Faithful are Blessed	189
Chapter 20	An Exalted View	201

INTRODUCTION

No Hurry to Horeb is the fourth volume in the *Ruminations on the Golden Strand Series*. The series encapsulate experiences gleaned during my faith walk and in the aftermath of spiritual transformation in following after the footsteps of Christ Jesus. There are also numerous insights and observations drawn from life's experiences that help to frame and present certain truths in a way that readers will find to be very interesting. Currently there are four volumes in the series with more planned for the future.

The journey of spiritual transformation is like climbing a mountain. It is not undertaken for bravado but to bring the seeker closer to the heart of divinity as he nears the summit. Many believers do have a genuine desire and make valiant efforts to complete the climb but often fall short. This book begins by pointing out that the mountain of faith turns out to be a very tall order for those that fail because they are not well informed about the nature and demands of God's call. Truth is the governing impulse of all things divine and the climb up God's mountain is the ultimate proofing in same. It is for good reason that spiritual transformation is equated to baptism in the fire of Truth. To love Truth is very costly in the world and has always been. The call up God's mountain is for those willing to live by Truth as well as pay the price for doing so no matter the cost in a world that holds little regard for it.

Introduction

Each time that mankind rejects Truth he makes accommodation for darkness and thereby loses a little bit of himself. He de-grades both himself and humanity as a whole in rejecting Truth for by doing so he disrupts the divine connection to God. Rejecting Truth is rejecting God because HE is Truth. The man that despises Truth has allowed a virus to infect the core of goodness within him. He has made room for a foreign species to invade the landscape of his mind to leave little room for the spirit of God to thrive. Truth may be bitter but it leaves a sweet after-taste in the mouth after all is done as said.

Mankind needs to understand how important it is to embrace Truth as a way of life. It is the difference between light that the world sorely lacks and darkness which encroaches everywhere. The man that lives by Truth has in essence dedicated his endeavors to God. His handiworks will be duly established for it will be well commended and infused with the divine essence. The work that has God's commendation will shine and draw praise from both the heavenly and earthly. On a cautionary note, he that does not live by Truth may profit in the short time but his earthly endeavors will not be well received above for God resists such. Mistruths and falsehood constitute a spiritual choke that deters goodness but Truth transforms and conditions every endeavor to abound in it.

It is next pointed out what great danger is posed when mankind chooses a life style that is keen to identify with the crowd or seeks to fit the popular mold. Choosing to go with the flow has become popular in today's world but it is a very slippery slope that should be rejected. Rather moderation in all areas of life needs to be chosen for it anchors the soul well. The importance of sacrifices voluntarily made in love must never be underestimated. Such helps to pare down the flesh and set the ego at naught so that the spirit within can fully abound. It is only when the spirit fully abounds that mankind is availed strong faith and great vision to be able to achieve a balance between the heavenly and earthly.

Strong faith and great vision are ingredients that combine to afford mankind the fullness of divine riches. He that remains ever blessed is he who understands that divine gifts are to be held in good custody and require diligent stewardship. The truly blessed man knows that to use life's blessings for noble service of humanity in sacrificial love is very pleasing to God. Such will be freed in spirit to join up with the Divine as well as availed the Holy Ghost to keep him informed and the Holy Spirit as helper.

The believer that is tuned in spirit to receive the gift of the Holy Ghost is able to know all things for he will be privy to conversations in heavenly places. It is the combination of information obtained by the Holy Ghost and power afforded through the Holy Spirit that makes all things to be possible through Christ. Those two are availed to the matured in spirit who are no longer just followers but have

Introduction

joined the congregation of the living church of Christ. The latter is the congregation of the mighty before God called to serve humanity in love through Christ.

Christ is a communion of the noble in spirit and the body a corporation of those willing to share with others in grace with love. It is a commonwealth of the justified before God that live by a heavenly mandate in accordance with God's will and are subject to laws that are higher than man's own. Only those that live by Truth and selfless love for all ever grow to full spiritual maturity to be called therein into Christ. It must be noted that no one is able to please God or be justified before him unless he has fully yielded for his divine will to direct his life. Such are kept apart to be fitted as vessels for works of divine glory.

The believer kept apart as a vessel of glory is not perfect for only God is but has entered into a perfecting process within the divine. The perfecting process is continuous and serves not only to custom fit but to affirm the truly faithful in Christ. It can be thought of as a time for the sizing of the signet ring of Providence and the measurement of the robe of eternity. It is like the purification of gold where there is an acceptable threshold to be met but absolute purity remains unattainable. The perfecting process entails continuous observations made from Heaven and relayed to the faithful below by the Holy Ghost so that such can become more like Christ in dealing with issues of life as he serves God's Divine purposes on earth.

Introduction

The glory of this world surely passes away but the gifts of God have great intrinsic and timeless value. Whereas the things of the world wane in value with the passage of time, divine gifts increase in value as the days unfold. The things of the world are about the present and localized. But the gifts of God are universal in nature, good today as well as for generations to come. Such gifts remain ever fulfilling, sustainable and enduring. Divine gifts are like true gold tried and purified in the fire of Truth with love. Such everlasting gifts bring fulfillment and are availed to the faithful who can soar in spirit to the exalted realm.

The exalted realm or heavenly places is the habitation of immortal souls where those that can rise in spirit to overcome the world congregate. The faithful believer able to ascend thither will have his heart beat in compassion as that of Christ and his mind connected to the mind of God. He that is so connected has become a son reborn in light and recreated in the image of Christ. He has become one fitted in spirit to carry out God's will always. He has joined an elect company and must stand to be counted worthy. He is one that has received the universal passport into the kingdom of light and must go beyond the gates for thereabouts is his portion. It has become appointed for him to step outside the box to excel in the glory ordained for those that have broken the chains of human mediocrity to become sons of light. He must learn to stand in good light always by overcoming his initial fears to venture beyond the known horizons.

Introduction

The kingdom of light is the field of dreams where the immortal spirits congregate for recreation. The recreation of immortals souls is to bring new things out of the old. It is their pride and joy to make sure that nothing worthy of salvage in creation is wasted for the Creator pronounced all that HE created to be good. The field of dreams is a place of amazement that is obscured to all but the pure of heart. It is the place of greater enlightenment revealed to only those that obey as God wills even as the dutiful child trusts and obeys the loving parent. It is the place of regeneration where the old things can be made new again.

There is a certain and definite order that governs everything in creation. That order was first set in place when God created the heavens, earth and everything contained therein. At the present time, it may all appear to be chaotic and confusing to the uninformed mind but looks are deceiving in this case. God did not set about to create confusion and chaos. He is never taken by surprise either for he knows all the way from the beginning through to the end of all things. It has to be clearly understood that regardless of how things look presently, at the end when it really counts most, the underlying order set down from the beginning by God will prevail.

God calls many to come up his mountain but there is a ledge two-thirds of the way up. Many who are called to come up God's mountain make it to the ledge but only a few are chosen to make it to the summit. The sons of God

Introduction

make it to the summit but the brides of Christ can only make it to the ledge. And so, the sons are connected to the three measures of the Trinity but the brides are only connected with the two measures of the Spirit and Son. Man has no choice in this matter for God is the final arbiter here. He knows the heart of everyone for he has made it so. He knows who will forsake all for his sake and who will forsake some but not all things. God is the potter and man is the clay. Nevertheless the Father still uses the brides of Christ to good effect in the work of his kingdom.

Truth makes for certainty of faith and affords spiritual strength to uphold the believer within. The word of God is the bread of life that duly turns into spiritual meat within as the faithful matures in the way of Christ. Therefore it is important for the believer to devote quality time to the study of the word of God as well as to prayer. The hour of prayer is the refueling stop for the spirit. It is the water break taken at the oasis of life by the weary traveler. The believer must drink regularly from the trough of the living water of the word else his spirit will atrophy.

This book is not a substitute for the Holy Bible but only serves to amplify the eternal truths contained therein. As the reader ruminates through this volume, I hope that the truth laid bare within the pages will help enlighten minds and reshape hearts into vessels of honor that live for Truth and love so that humanity can become collectively better.

Kalu Onwuka

Eagle that walks wobbly on earth

Is at home in the exalted heights

Where majesty is very becoming

And nothing is hidden from view

Chapter 1

A PLACE ON THE MOUNTAIN

Regardless of the faith that he subscribes to, every seeker desires to connect in spirit with the deity that is the object of his devotion. In the Christian faith, the true believer who desires to make this connection must follow the path laid down and modeled by Christ Jesus. It is a path that leads man's spirit upwards to the mountain top of faith. Most Christians congregate at the base of the mountain and are content or resigned to camp out there. But the base of the mountain is not for camping out. The base is where the call to come up the mountain can be heard most clearly. Many heed the call to come up the mountain in order to find true fulfillment thereby. Such make valiant efforts but end up on a ledge two-thirds of the way up the mountain without reaching the summit. It is not the top but a place of resorting so that only the truly committed few out of the many can continue to the summit.

Most who reach the ledge of hope camp out there and can go no further. They fall short of the desired goal of reaching the mountain top. They fall short because they are not able to let go of some things that they have brought up the face of the mountain with them. These are earthly possessions that they treasure but which belong in the past and are not needed in the kingdom of light at the summit. Nevertheless the believers that hang out at the ledge are used by God as ministers of the gospel of the Christ for a given season and up to a certain extent. However a few are willing to let go of everything without counting cost so that they can make it to the top. These will become the christened in light and covenant sons of the heavenly Father that inherit the kingdom.

The few who make it to the top are the ones who have truly followed in the footsteps of the Christ Jesus to overcome the world. Such have become fully matured in the spirit of Christ to join the congregation of the living church that congregate at the summit. They will come to know the mysteries of the kingdom of light and the hidden things concerning God. It takes a full commitment and total dedication to climb to the summit of God's mountain. It is not for everyone but for those called to do so in spirit by God. It is for those who have been chosen for life everlasting and eternal habitation with the heavenly Father. They are chosen to be duly adopted as sons under God's mercy and to be bestowed with divine wisdom as secrets of the family business.

The Christian bible is a book of symbolism that contains

hidden truths that have to be searched out and known by spiritual discernment. Certain truths can be discerned from the epistle letters of the Apostles Paul when studied carefully. There is an orderliness which can be observed from the book of Romans through to the book of Thessalonians. Each book relates to the different stages of the climb up God's mountain. The book of Romans publishes the reality of God, the debased nature of man and God's plan for the redemption of mankind by transforming his spirit through Christ. The books of the Corinthians expound on the why, who, how, what, when and where of that spiritual transformation. The books serve to bring conclusion to the known old ways of Moses and publish the general outline of the emerging new way of the Christ. The underlying theme there is that the follower must climb God's mountain after Christ who has shown the way. Along the way up that mountain, the seeker will be helped up and protected by grace afforded by those who are ahead of him. As he climbs up, it is required of him to afford the same help in grace to others that follow after him. It is by this giving to lift others up in the way that seekers after Christ come to abound in him.

It helps to think of the books of the Corinthians as a travel brochure or rather a mountain guide. The books contain information and tips that the climber needs to know so that he can be successful in his quest to ascend to the summit. It points out how to locate the mountain, tools needed and how to get there among other useful tips. It makes accommodation for all who will venture up the mountain including those who will never reach the top. The book of Romans defines the mission of Christ but that of the Corinthians serve as a prospectus to prepare the would-be follower on what to expect on the trail of Christ up God's mountain as well as what to gain at the top. The would-be follower must be well-informed so that he can determine for himself whether to take up God's offer or not. He must not be like the builder of the tower that starts to build and could not complete the task because he failed to determine what was needed beforehand.

The book of Galatians relates to the foothills of the mountain of God. It is about all the believers who have received the information about God's offer and have gathered around the foothills of his mountain. They are like travelers who have left the old and unfulfilling to seek out the place of new promise. The new place looks very strange and is very discomforting for them. They must learn to communicate in a new language, dress in different ways and eat different foods. It is a struggle to get used to the new for the familiar ways of the old still call. In other words, the mountain of God looms forbidding and insurmountable to those that are gathered around its foothills. Many will remain there for they are not able to let go of the old ways so that they can begin to fully explore the new. They will turn the campgrounds of the foothills into their permanent dwellings. They have already failed even before they started. They know about God's words and his promises but they have not been changed in any way. They may look the part of the followers of Christ but they will not be changed within where it matters most.

God's word of Truth declares that with him the impossible becomes possible for mankind. The seeker that accepts this declaration to be true, turns his back on the old way and takes his first faltering steps up that mountain is the Ephesian. He has courageously battled the demons of his old life through faith in Christ Jesus so that a new life begins to emerge in him. The old self is a dogged fighter that does not give up easily. However he finds more than his match in Christ Jesus. With each step that the believer takes, the new self gets stronger and the old self gets weaker. He that dares to climb finds that the inner self is revitalized in the air up God's mountain. The revitalizing agent is the spirit of God. The Spirit of God is a flyer that is easily airborne but the flesh is a crawler that revels in the dust of the earth. The new self is guided by the spirit which helps him up the mountain whereas the old debased self is led by the flesh which keeps him earthbound.

The book of Ephesians relates to the victory of the emerging new self over the old dying self. It deals with the first concrete steps that the true believer takes up the mountain in his quest for eternal life and communion with the Divine up at the summit. As such, the book of Ephesians represents the place where the believer comes to make a full commitment to the way of Christ. He must do so in order to continue his transformation in spirit from the debased lowly state of the old to a purified exalted state of the new. This is where the believer begins to settle in Christ and grow roots that will sustain him in the way. He will begin to have experiences of the Divine due to the awakening spirit within him. Life begins to have a new meaning and purpose for the spirit now leads him towards purer light. He can see his way better in life. He no longer drifts and casts about in the world without true purpose or to please others. Rather all his steps become ordered and lead up the mountain. He will come to abound in the grace of God through Christ for he is on his way to rendezvous with destiny and the Divine. It is here that he will become enamored with Truth and cannot be filled enough with the teachings of Christ Jesus.

The teachings of Christ Jesus serve to reassure the believer as he learns and keeps them in his heart. God's promises of redemption for the sinner, his love for mankind, his wisdom and power to do the amazing as well as the hymns of worship bring much delight to his soul. The seeker will begin to experience and understand the full implication of the grace of God through Christ. He will realize that Christ is all about sharing and that fellowship with Christ is to become part of that which lives not for self but for the welfare and benefit of all. For the seeker at this stage, it becomes as if a candle has been lit in his heart and he is being led in the same direction as others with similarly lit hearts. The testimony of the words of Christ Jesus which the follower has kept and nourished in his heart is the candle. The flame will remain lit as long as the seeker lives in accordance with the Truth treasured in his heart.

As life here begins to take on a new and different meaning for the believer, a brighter dawn of understanding will break out will for him. This brighter dawn brings a strengthening of faith and deeper spiritual understanding in the inner man about God's ways. The believer has reached the stage where he is being immersed in the consciousness of the Divine. This can only come about where there is genuine love for God and reverence for his laws. The Spirit of God searches the heart of man and is able to determine where there is true or feigned love for him. The heart that has fully committed to love God will be open for his Spirit to come in and start pouring in the 'potion' of the Divine. It is akin to downloading from an infinite divine source to a finite earthly receiver. It takes up to seventeen years to reach a certain critical threshold of spiritual maturity. However it is a perfecting process that never really ends and continues well beyond that threshold within the Divine fold.

The believer that has the Spirit of God to guide him in life will increase in spiritual knowledge and understanding. Out of the chaos of life will begin to crystallize an orderliness and purpose that mirrors God's promises in the scriptures. The believer so guided will become aware that he now lives under the will of God and that the Holy

Bible is a place to find answers to life's daily problems. He will realize that he has changed a lot in the spirit within so much that his flesh nature can only exercise minimal control over him. He will begin to understand his true place in God's creation and that he is not alone but part of a spiritual nation. He will soon discover that he is not just flesh but something far greater in God through Christ Jesus. He has turned into a new creature in God that will in due time grow into the spiritual image of God. Indeed, he has found the true way of life through the light of Christ.

It takes some time to become fully committed to God but gradually the believer will learn to do so and come to trust God with all his heart. He will become tuned to hear and trust the voice of the spirit within that in essence urges him to let go of all his worries and let God handle them. This is where he learns to trust God and to lean less on his own understanding. He will also learn that it serves the follower well to acknowledge God and be thankful for all that he has for thereby he will abound in more. He is now on his way to victory but he must learn to put on the full armor of the spiritual warrior for he has become a target of the prince of darkness. He needs to put on the full armor so that he can make gainful strides in his way up God's mountain. The full armor is like the protective gear and harnesses that the climber needs. This is because the enemy will seek ways to hinder and bring the faithful follower who has made gainful strides back down to earth.

The prince of darkness of this world who is the enemy of light perceives where the flame of Christ has been lit in the heart and will battle to put it out. This is an arena of constant spiritual battling for the follower after Christ but God makes provision so that such can be victorious. God always delivers the faithful and makes a way for him during this time of spiritual struggle. There is no other way to grow in faith than to go through the gauntlet. It is the only way to be rid of fear and doubt. There is no better way for God to affirm his reality than to allow the follower to pass through such trials. God will usually send needed help through one further along in spiritual maturity to inspire, guide, encourage and intercede through prayer for the seeker in this season of his spiritual life. The helper sent is the believer ahead of him in the climb to whom it can be likened that he is tethered to with a life rope. In time the follower so helped will learn to do the same for the climber behind him. This helping of the weaker by the stronger in faith is a powerful demonstration of grace through Christ that must govern the life of every believer.

Not only must the believer put on the protective gear and harnesses that is his full armor of battle but he must never put it off once he has put it on for he has joined God's team. The enemy of light uses countless ways to try to extinguish the flame that has been lit in the heart of the believer at this juncture. These include the alluring bait of the old way of wanton living accusations, manipulation, mockery, and derision. Such is the age old battle of evil against goodness or darkness against light. As long as the seeker is on the face of the mountain climbing up, he will be a beacon of light that others below can see and aim to join. In order to remain that beacon up the mountain that others can see to join, he must love and embrace Truth regardless of cost. It is the only way to remain watchful and guard well the flame of love for God that burns in the heart through Christ. He that remains faithful in the way and diligent in his watch will have his heart become an altar of the heavenly Father in due season.

Truth is insurance that protects the climber and brings him good rewards for his efforts. The agents of darkness pose as messengers of light but in reality aim to beguile the unwary into a downfall. The only escape from this is to love Truth unconditionally. He that does so will have nothing to hide and nothing can be hidden from him for Truth searches to reveal all things. The love of Truth exacts much toll but it costs only those things that are not needed in the climb. It may not be understood beforehand but it will come to be later as the climber ascends up the mountain. He will discover that the earthly things that he lost along the way were obstacles that needed to be discarded in order to ease his climb as only the streamlined in spirit can ascend to the exalted heights.

Chapter Highlights

- ✓ Many make good efforts to climb God's mountain but only a few make a full commitment.
- ✓ A place on the mountain top is appointed for those who have been chosen for eternal life with God.
- ✓ Seekers should know about the sacrifices required before starting the climb up God's mountain.
- ✓ It takes a great struggle to get used to the new way of Christ when the old and familiar ways still call.
- ✓ The old-self is a dogged fighter and does not yield easily except with divine intercession.
- ✓ The walk of faith is a series of steps that leads up to a spiritual rendezvous with Christ in due time.
- ✓ There is an orderliness and purpose in life that results when the believer has true love for God.
- ✓ It takes time to become fully committed to God and learn to trust his words of promises.
- ✓ The prince of darkness perceives where the flame of Christ has been lit and will seek to put it out.
- ✓ The climber that is on the face of God's mountain will be a beacon for others below to follow.
- ✓ The prince of darkness poses as a messenger of light in order to beguile the unwary into a downfall.
- ✓ The climb up the mountain of faith removes the cluttering not needed in the kingdom of light.

The flame of love highlights the way

In ascents and descents up the ladder

As twinkling lights in the stream of life

To and fro between Heaven and earth

Chapter 2

MUSTERING FOR THE GOOD FIGHT

The full armor of God helps to assure victory as the faithful makes his spiritual ascent up God's mountain. It helps the believer to understand the spiritual symbolism and significance of its many distinct parts so as to leave no room for the enemy to hurt him. As mentioned in the previous chapter, Truth is the foundational armor which affords protection for the pure of heart. Fellowship with Christ begins and ends with Truth. God is a Spirit and they that worship him must worship in spirit and in Truth. Christ Jesus came to rescue those who love Truth and only they can truly embrace his message. Spiritual connection or communion with the heavenly Father can only be made through Truth and love for all. The believer must be truthful in every area of life so as to remain pure in the spirit within and of good use to God. He that loves Truth will meet up with Christ and the heavenly Father duly.

Only those that love Truth can 'see' the way into God's playing field. The latter is much sought after for it is where the good and perfect abound. He that loves Truth will always harvest good fruits from all his endeavors for God will always be at hand for him. The believer that covers every area of his life in Truth will be rewarded with desirable outcomes for he will be guided by the Holy Spirit. He that is so guided will not produce the 'sterile' but will receive good fruits for his labor as the Holy Spirit is a harbinger of life. The loin symbolizes the instrument that man uses to produce fruits or such works that have life within. The faithful believer that covers his loin with Truth will produce good works. His handiworks will have life in that they will be sustainable, fulfilling and enduring.

The handiwork that is covered by Truth is in essence dedicated to God and will be established in its due time. This is because God is Truth and the work that is carried out in truth is infused with the Spirit of life. The work that has God's commendation or his hand in it will shine and evoke praise from men for the heavenly Father. On a cautionary note, the loin is a vulnerable point where the enemy attempts to choke to death all the good works that man intends to produce. The professed believer that does not love Truth will choke his good work. Mistruths and the false constitute a spiritual choke that aborts goodness but truth works to condition and enhance same.

God did not create man with a disobedient heart or put the impulse in him to speak mistruths and tell lies to his fellow man. It is true that the spirit of the world is a lie that masquerades as Truth. Yet the tendency to tell lies and misrepresent things is an acquired taste that is unnatural to man. Mankind has a tendency to go astray only when he sees others doing so. No one likes to take the first plunge or be the first in line to break the rule but most will follow suit after observing the first transgressor. It stems from the compulsive tendency of man to identify with the crowd and not be seen as the odd one. The enemy of light exploits this tendency by using his agents to initiate that first act of disobedience or trespass. After that first act, it becomes much easier to get the rest to follow along. It is the same ploy that he used in the paradise of Eden and continues to use in the world today.

It is a game changer in life when man learns to say no to the crowd and yes to the word of Truth. This is a major milestone in spiritual transformation and represents the turnaround point where the spread of darkness is halted. As such, it represents the turning point where the works of darkness begins to be counter-acted and the curse of Eden lifted. It is from this turning point that man can begin to journey towards Eden where he can commune with God as it once was. It is from this point when he has learned to say no to the world and yes to Truth that mankind can continue his upward climb on God's mountain. On the top of God's mountain rests mankind's chance to recreate Eden. On the top of God's mountain is where the faithful obtains the 'clean slate' to fashion a pristine lifestyle to reflect the divine presence that dwells within him.

The man that is not yet awakened in his spirit is likely to follow suit and transgress as he sees others committing the same follies. He is the un-informed man who does not yet realize that he is following a time beaten track path that has been laid out by the prince of the darkness of the world. It is a pathway that leads to further estrangement between man and his Creator. The Spirit of God desires and hopes for reconciliation with man by transforming him in spirit. However the prince of darkness works ceaselessly to prevent that from taking place. He poses as mankind's friend but aims to forestall the spiritual transformation and communion with God that is man's appointed destiny.

The prince of darkness swindles mankind of his precious time on earth as he beguiles the unwary into doing things that work to estrange him further from God. It is precious time that mankind can better devote to seeking after Christ so that he can understand God and self. Only when that comes about can he come to know the reason for his brief existence on earth. The prince of the darkness of this world is the enemy of God that has been cast down and banished from the place of honor that he once occupied with God. For that reason, he is determined to do all in his power to prevent mankind from having what he once had but cannot have anymore. And so for the enemy, it is really a case of if I cannot have it then no one else can.

The believer that has started the climb up the mountain of faith has been somewhat awakened in spirit. He may not be fully awake but he is no longer asleep. He will no longer be swindled of his precious time on earth by the enemy but begin to invest his time in the worthwhile. He will no longer crave or long to belong with the crowd but care more for goodness and to please God. He may be in the world but he will become increasingly less enamored of it for he has found a more fulfilling way. The way that he has found is the path of righteousness.

The believer that is being led on the path of righteousness has to be pure of heart in his dealings with humanity in order to remain there. Righteousness is of the heart and must determine all of mankind's intentions and actions. The righteous man does all things for goodness sake so that God may be pleased and not for men's praise. He is not motivated by self-interest or personal gain. All his acts are governed by goodwill and the desire for the welfare of all. All his acts of charity are offered up as burnt sacrifice to God so that in that way he can lay up treasure in heavenly places. Treasure laid up in Heaven translates into goodness and mercy that will come to follow the faithful in his time of need as he lives out his time on earth. The believer whose heart truly desires to please God will know the things to do that will be well commended by the heavenly Father. By the same token, he will also come to know in his heart the things that will displease God.

Where there is no true love for God, man will end up doing things aimed at soliciting praise from men for self instead of seeking to bring praise and due glory to God. Praise for the heavenly Father becomes an afterthought and a matter of formality when one craves men's praise. Such only bloats the ego and leads man to be stalled in his spiritual growth. His outside appearance may look becoming but he will be empty in the inner man of the spirit where God meets man. Unbridled ego leads mankind to become an overgrown bush that bears no good fruit. The sweet smelling fragrance of the offering well received by God will be missing in his life. He will lack the anointing of God and the aroma of eternity will not follow in his wake. His works will amount to nothing more than a filthy rag with which he will attempt to cover his spiritual nakedness. All his undertakings on earth will turn out to be dead works for he will never receive the commendation of God for the job well done. He will be precluded from coming to maturity in Christ for he is unfaithful in the way.

The believer who serves God in faithfulness will become a favorite target of the prince of the darkness of this world. He will become the focus of constant attacks so as to stop him from continuing in righteous works borne out of love for God and humanity. All works of righteousness are touched by the divine hand and so shine before men. The shine of the divine touch angers the prince of the darkness of this world to no end. It is the touch of love and commendation for work well done that he can never have. It is this envy that drives the enemy to oppose such works that please the soul and draw mankind towards true light.

It is important that the faithful learn to cover the feet with the message of peace regardless of the attacks of the enemy. The feet symbolize the vehicle that takes man places on earth. Wherever the righteous of heart traverses on earth, he has to do so in peace as he fulfills his calling. It is only by peace that the faithful can be productive and of good service to God. It is only when he is at peace that he can hear the still small voice of the divine that guides him. It is the hallmark of every faithful believer that he leaves a trail of enlightenment in the wake of his earthly walk. Enlightenment is a sprinkling of the divine ethos and serves to show mankind how God would like to have things done on earth. Every believer that is led by the Divine cannot help but leave the footprints and handprints of Christ along his earthly path.

In order to remain at peace and at rest in God while facing ceaseless attacks in the world, the faithful has to learn to build up his reservoir of spiritual strength. This comes about by constantly feeding on the word of Truth and writing them on the tablet of the heart. The word of Truth written in the heart must guide and cover every aspect of daily life. He that lives in accordance with Truth will be availed the spiritual strength necessary to overcome the attacks directed at him. It will afford him the tools to prevail in his times of crises for the words that he has fed on will nourish him in trials. It turns out that spiritual meat is borne of God's Truth that the believer feeds on.

Spiritual meat within the believer translates into spiritual strength needed to withstand the attacks of the prince of darkness but also to understand the divine mysteries. It is deeper knowledge and understanding of the hidden that affords the faithful the peace that allows him to thrive in a troublesome world. As he encounters and overcomes each trouble, his faith in God's ability to fulfill all that he has promised will also increase. It is by the shield of faith that he will make necessary accommodation for divine gifts to abound in his life as well as be shielded from the envious attacks of the enemy that they attract. He that has strapped on the shield of faith is in safe hands as long as he continues to trust God without wavering.

It takes spiritual strength within to enable the faithful believer to hold up the shield of faith through his times of troubles. It is same that enables him to prevail during his battles with the enemy and to bring up the spiritual child within to manhood. The faithful whose spirit within has grown to full maturity in Christ has passed the test of faith. Such has been salvaged from a debased to a purified state through Christ to become a clean vessel prepared and ready to be used for work by God.

Chapter Highlights

- ✓ Truth is the foundational armor that affords protection to those who walk in the way of Christ.
- ✓ Truth leads the believer to abound in good fruits and protects him from producing dead works.
- ✓ The handiwork that is true and pure will be duly established for such is dedicated to God in essence.
- ✓ The compulsive tendency of the faithless to identify with the crowd leads to dishonor of Truth.
- ✓ A clean slate to fashion a pristine life that reflects the divine essence is obtained through Christ.
- ✓ The believer on the climb up God's mountain sees his time on earth as precious and uses it wisely.
- ✓ The acts of charity offered up as burnt sacrifices serve to lay up treasures in heavenly places.
- ✓ The seeker who seeks praise from men rather than God's approval will be stalled in spiritual growth.
- ✓ The works of righteousness shine before men for such are well commended by the Divine.
- ✓ The matured in Christ bring enlightenment and a sprinkling of the divine ethos on earth.
- ✓ The believer that has been found and redeemed must go back and help find those lost in the way.
- ✓ The believer that has been nurtured in spirit from infancy to full maturity is a much treasured vessel.

The true essence of godliness

Is endurance that lasts 'til end

And love that seeks for the best

In hope matured through faith

Chapter 3

WINNING NEW GROUNDS

For the maturing believer to be an effective player on offense and win new souls for God, the sword of the spirit is availed to him. The new in Christ inevitably plays defense on God's team for a good while until full maturity. Therefore it takes some time to come to the reality of the sword of the spirit and take it up. The sword of the spirit enables the fully matured in Christ to speak out words that bring insight and shed light on all matters that he will encounter on his way. He that takes up the sword of the spirit in good faith becomes an earthly mouthpiece for knowledge and wisdom that originates from behind the throne of the heavenly Father. This is knowledge that applies to specific persons and situations where God desires change. It is knowledge that addresses the ugly that lurks hidden in men's hearts so that such can be rid and replaced with better. It is knowledge used to break down stony hearts and reform them into vessels of hope.

Only the fully matured In Christ can be entrusted with the sword of the spirit by the heavenly Father. Only the believer that is willing to go where God sends and speak out Truth in good faith can wield the sword. Most men recoil from Truth borne of the sword and others are offended by it for it bares all things naked in light. It should be kept in mind that man's ego works to oppose the spirit and mislead him to presume to be right. He who wields the sword has been engaged to fight God's battles and need not be concerned with how Truth is received. He is only there to serve the will of the Father who has pre-ordained everything. He is only there to lend his mind and body for the battle is fought in the spirit of the living God.

The sword of Truth is a very powerful spiritual weapon that tears through the defenses that man attempts to put up against it. Truth is sharp when wielded by the noble in spirit but blunt in the hands of the profane. The sword of truth offers up words that do not return void but accomplish the things for which there are spoken. God is in control of all things even though it may not always seem that way to the faithless. In order to remain anchored in faith and not be misled by the look of things, the believer must never neglect to pray, study, fast and give due thanks to God. It is the only way that the he can remain at peace in the spirit within and be tuned to hear when the Spirit of God speaks to his heart.

The faithful that embraces Christ in good faith, loves truth, harbors goodwill and seeks to live peaceably with all men will prove to be a dependable warrior for God. Such a warrior battles for light and must remain unwavering in his trust of God regardless of circumstances. He must never shrink from speaking boldly as moved by the Divine. He that battles for God in this light will be appropriately suited to stand up to the forces of evil and be victorious in his earthly endeavors. He will bear good fruits in all areas of life for God will always be near and at hand for him. Being a faithful warrior for God affords a connection that makes the believer a special vessel whose pleas and petitions are readily heard because he lives to serve God.

God will always answer the prayers and make provision for the needs of the faithful warrior on his team who battle valiantly for Truth. Sometimes the answer or solution to the problem may not come about when expected and at other times it may come about in unexpected ways. Nevertheless, God's answers always suffice for his ways are different from men's and prove to be far better in the long run. The faithful that petitions for his needs to be met must be on the lookout for how the supply will be met for God often works in ways that are mysterious to mankind. The petitioner should keep in mind that God always looks for different means and uses every occasion possible to reveal new dimensions and hitherto unknown aspects about the divine way. It is by so doing that HE exposes new veins of the divine gold for the seeker to mine as well as help the faith of believers to become stronger.

The prayers of the spiritual warrior should not only be for

personal needs but should be intercessory also. The way of Christ is about giving of oneself so that the lot can be better. It takes the sacrifice of one to make the rest better. It is the measure of leaven that enhances the whole meal. Christ is about seeking the wealth of all in a spiritual commonwealth. Much good comes about when the believer prays for his needs as well as those of others to be met. It speaks to the compassion that defines the heart of Christ Jesus. In praying for the needs of others, the faithful shares in their burden. When the faithful share in the burden and suffering of others, it hastens God's response for he hates to see his beloved faithful suffer needlessly. Unbeknown to the believer, whenever he includes others in his prayers others will in turn include him in theirs. It is the law of the harvest of the good seed sown. Every good deed carried out in love for the welfare of humanity is always rewarded many times over in God's economy. It should be noted that the garden of love yields a bountiful harvest for those that labor in righteousness for humanity.

Often times while the believer makes intercessory prayer for those who are younger in faith or just starting the climb up God's mountain, he neglects to pray for those who are his elders in faith. These are the faithful who are much further along in their climb or more matured in Christ. Some may have reached the top of the mountain of God but others may not be there quite yet. Such are the saintly in spirit who have maintained and kept open the trail blazed by Christ Jesus so that others too can follow after them up the way. It is highly necessary and beneficial that the 'follower' remember to pray for the elders that have preceded him in faith. The spirits of the saints are eternally alive as flames alight in God's love that line up the trail ahead so that followers after them are kept from stumbling. Their spirits line the trail up God's mountain to whisper encouragement to the weary climber as he inches up the lofty heights. In praying for the less or his contemporaries in the climb of faith, the believer is spiritually giving them his greetings. But in praying for those who have gone before him or higher up in the climb, he is spiritually giving them his salutation. The faithful should always send down greetings to the up and coming but he must also send up salutation to the elders in faith.

Salutation recognizes and acknowledges that which is superior. When the superior is duly recognized and acknowledged, the way up is made much easier for the faithful. The spirits of the saints hear the faithful believer as he prays for them. In praying for them, the believer joins up his faith with those of the saints for the fellowship of Christ is a communion of spirits. As the faithful believer prays for the saints, he gains spiritual access and attains that which he is not able to do by himself. The spirits of the saints are always in communion as one in prayer for and within the flock of Christ Jesus. It bodes well for the faithful believer to connect with the saintly in spirit by praying for them for the prayers of such rise unimpeded to reach God's ears instantly.

Only the saintly in spirit can reach the top of God's mountain. Every saintly soul has reached the purest and highest state of spiritual transformation that is possible for base man. They have pared the flesh to the minimum so that the spirit within can abound to the utmost to have complete sway over them. Being that God's word is a burden often heavier than most can bear, the saints can assist and help the believer to serve God far more exceedingly than they can on their own. The saints are like the heavy lifters in God's kingdom who the believer can leverage to move things that are too burdensome for them. They shine greater light and point out ways where none seems to exist. Having reached the top of faith-mountain, the saintly in spirit can show the willing believer how to scale the last foreboding heights.

The saints can help the faithful in Christ change the earthly landscape for better for humanity. They can help to show mankind ways to bring about needed changes and advance the kingdom of God on earth. The saints can be thought of as spiritual Fathers that carry young ones on their shoulders so that they can have less fear, become more perceptive and learn to use all the spiritual tools available to them. The believer who prays for and holds the saints in blessed memory will partake of the portion of goodness and mercy divinely appointed for them.

Chapter Highlights

- ✓ The sword of the Spirit is afforded the matured in faith so that he can win new grounds for God.
- ✓ He that is willing to go where God sends and speak in faithfulness will wield the sword of the spirit.
- ✓ The sword of Truth is sharp when wielded by the noble in spirit but blunt in hands that profane it.
- ✓ The greatest asset of the believer that battles for God in goodness is the power of his prayers.
- ✓ God uses different means and occasions to reveal himself to those that walk on the righteous path.
- ✓ The believer that shares in the burden of others will have God respond to meet his own needs.
- ✓ It is necessary for the faithful to pray not only for the young but also for the elders in faith.
- ✓ Praying for the elders in faith allows the believer to attain things that he is not able to do by himself.
- ✓ The elders have scaled faith-mountain and know how to use spiritual tools availed through Christ.
- ✓ The saintly bring good gifts from the heavenly to earthly places so that those that lack can have.
- ✓ He that has the gift of the Holy Ghost takes every step in the light of knowledge and wisdom.
- ✓ The saintly shine a greater light and help to point out the way where none seems to exist.

The sweet endearing hours of prayer

In cherished songs and diligent study

Are golden moments when Heaven

Opens its window to cheerful delight

Chapter 4

CALL TO THE SUMMIT

Fulfillment and earthly bliss can only come about as mankind realizes the fullness of the riches of God. The believer that comes to realize such fullness is the one who understands that the gifts of God require diligent stewardship and are to be held in trust for the welfare of humanity. He that uses life's blessings to serve all in goodness and love is a faithful servant deemed worthy of divine gifts. There are two roads in life. One is the broad and hurried way which most follow. It is the road preferred by those who rely on their own understanding, power and might. Such that follow this darkening path which entombs men's souls and leads to spiritual death have neither fear nor love for God. All who walk on that path will never be free in spirit to join the conversation in heavenly places but remain bound to the earthly.

However there is another path on which the righteous before God walk. It is the path of Christ and the road less traveled where only a few are found. Although it is a narrow and confining trail, yet it is the path ordained for the faithful who love to obey the will of the heavenly Father. Although few in number the followers of this path thrive in the light, knowledge and love of God. It is a path that requires the follower to tarry sometimes for the Holy Spirit to lead in his earthly endeavors. It demands that the believer wait for direction and go where the Spirit of God points. Those that follow this path come to be enlightened in mind, mature in spirit and have their footsteps guided in divine light. This righteous path is for those called in spirit by God and demands a rejection of the world's way.

Although many who are called to God's way respond initially, a good number abandon the calling and drift away from its path. The events and circumstances narrated in the last chapter of the gospel of John that involves the Apostle Peter and six other disciples provide a good case study of the believer who nearly abandons his calling. When the calling is abandoned, the erstwhile believer reverts to the habits and old ways that had previously proven to be unfulfilling for him. On the other hand, the believer who remains faithful and perseveres in his calling will be come into spiritual communion with the Divine. It is through perseverance and faithfulness that the heavenly and earthly come to merge as one to God's glory. He in whom the heavenly and earthly find accord will project God's will on earth to have fulfillment in body and soul.

In the last chapter of the gospel of John referenced above, the scene that is set on the shores of Lake Tiberias finds

Peter and some select disciples of Christ Jesus. They have arrived at life's crossroads and are not quite sure how to proceed. The men look up to the Apostle Peter for guidance to help them figure out what steps to take next. Peter may not yet realize it but he has been divinely ordained as the one that the men will follow as he leads. Therefore as he decides to go fishing, they all decide to come along too. But sadly he has decided to cast about for the wrong fish of worldly material instead of the real fish of the souls of men. His decision will take them down the darkened path where all of man's undertakings lead to nothing and result in futility. To abandon the path that the believer has been called to, leads to the night time of spiritual life. But to continue on the righteous path and remain true to God's calling, leads the faithful to do the work of glory that has been divinely ordained for him on earth. He that is faithful to his calling in the light of Christ will always find purpose, fulfillment and meaning in life.

The instruction given by Christ Jesus to the disciples as he departed was that they should gather in Jerusalem and remain joined in spirit through prayer to await a special gift to be dispensed from Heaven. It turns out that this gift will be the Holy Ghost who brings the key of knowledge that reveals the hidden. The Holy Ghost is the medium that affords access to knowledge that is hidden behind the veil of the heavenly throne. It affirms spiritual transformation and connects the faithful believer with God in spirit. It is the universal medium that the heavenly

Father uses to communicate with his own. It sets apart those who have been established through grace unto mercy. The realm of mercy is a place of infinite possibilities appointed for those matured in Christ. It is the realm wherein God sheds his glory on the faithful that have been willing to give up much for love of Truth and goodness. The door of mercy is opened to the merciful in spirit so that they can glimpse that which is hidden behind the veil. The merciful are the noble in spirit who will always share what they know or have.

The Apostle Peter was not following the instruction of Christ Jesus when he went fishing instead of tarrying in Jerusalem. Therefore he was not living in the will of the Father but in his own. Everyone who will come into fulfillment in Christ will inevitably pass through this period of hesitation. It is the pause before the unknown door through which one has never passed before. For a season in his faith walk, Peter yielded to the call of his past life. He will once again encounter the inevitable dead end that he had once escaped when he answered the initial call to follow Christ Jesus. But it is by this momentary lapse in judgment that Peter will be called again by the Master into a better light of understanding. But he will respond for good the second time as the sheep that hears the Master's voice. He will reset his life in accordance with God's will and thereby fulfill his divine calling. He will be transformed to become a building block of the kingdom of light in due season to lead others therein through Christ.

The same question asked by Christ on the shores of Lake Tiberias faces every believer that follows in the light after his footsteps today. The shore of Lake Tiberias represents the place of the baptism in the spirit of the fire of God. It is that which separates the eternal from the earthbound. It is the point of demarcation between that which will escape death and that which will not. The question posed by Christ about having meat is not about food for the belly but about spiritual fortitude. God asks this question and waits for an answer from every believer that he intends to use for the work of his kingdom. Did you eat, keep and share the bread of life as broken down and offered to you through grace so that you can have the meat of the Divine spirit in you is the question posed here.

The bread of life is of course the word of God as embodied in the teachings of Christ Jesus. The true follower has the words of Truth written in his heart to live in accordance by them. He shares the word of life with others so that they too can come into the knowledge of God. It is through this process of feeding and sharing that one comes into an intimate knowledge of God. It requires spiritual meat or fortitude for the believer to come into an intimate knowledge of God through Christ as there are many challenges to overcome along the way. In not obeying the Master's instruction to tarry in Jerusalem, Peter and his companion inevitably entered into a season of spiritual famine and doubt. It is during spiritual famine engendered by neglecting to feed on the word of Truth that the unfaithful in the way come to lack the meat of the spirit and be disconnected from God's will as fear and doubt set in to encumber the soul.

In that brief interlude, the Apostle Peter regressed spiritually into Simon the fisherman who lives in the limited understanding borne of spiritual famine. He went back to relying on his own power and might instead of letting the spirit of God work through him to accomplish his goals. To tarry in Jerusalem means to remain in a place of internal peace that comes from total trust in God. But to cast about in one's own will robs the follower after Christ of internal peace. Peter no longer lived by faith but relied on his flawed judgment. He had gone back to do that which seems good to the eye but proves futile in the end. He has to relearn to live by faith. His faith has to be revitalized to live by the word of Truth and trust in the unfailing promises of God to sustain him till the end.

It is in trusting and living by the word of Truth through Christ that the starving spirit is replenished with spiritual meat. The believer that is so replenished will have the power of God available for him to use to change his surroundings and course of events in life for better. The bereft and hopeless situation in life will be reversed to become fruitful yet again with the power of God availed. The faithful that is fortified with spiritual meat will have the power of God show forth mightily in him to accomplish works of glory in his life. But where spiritual meat or fortitude is lacking, the famished believer is left to strive on his own power and might without God's power to aid. Such that labors on his own will not afford the fulfilling, sustainable and enduring in life for the odds to succeed will be greatly against him.

He that is famished in spirit lives in a spiritual night time. The night time is not meant for doing great works by the mankind. Rather it is time that God uses to warn, teach and prepare the willing for the task ahead. It is a season for the believer to learn more about the words and ways of the Divine. It is a time when the believer will progress from lesser to greater enlightenment about the Divine. The knowledge and wisdom that is received in the spiritual night time is necessary in preparing the believer for victory in his walk of faith at dawn's break. It also affords the spiritual experience and grounding in faith that will help the believer to testify about the goodness of God to others later. There is always wonder working power when the good news of Christ borne of true testimony is shared with mankind. God is Truth and it is by true witnessing that divine power is mightily displayed among mankind.

Spiritual growth is never limited nor does it take place in a vacuum. The faithful believer is himself changed as he labors to change others for God and goodness. There is always some flock to be fed and lost sheep to be found. This is the calling of all who profess to follow in the footsteps of Christ Jesus. The calling is simply to receive from God in the light of Truth and to share with men in love. The believer who understands and faithfully answers this call will grow to full maturity in Christ. He will be transformed in spirit to be lifted close to the heart of God. He will become a true spiritual copy of Christ Jesus. He that is so changed has become a son of God bestowed with the mind of Christ. The mind of Christ knows and obeys the will of the heavenly Father. The faithful that has become christened in this way receives due knowledge and is directed in spirit from heavenly places. Such is one duly informed in mind by the Holy Ghost and guided in footsteps by the Holy Spirit who no longer lives for self but goes about faithfully on earth for the heavenly Father.

The Apostle Peter and his companion disciples had not completed the process of spiritual transformation yet. They had come to the ledge but had not yet reached the summit of God's mountain which was the place of his true calling. The ledge is the place where the faithful tarry for a while so that God can sort out who will make it to the summit and who will not. The faithful who are willing to forsake fame and fortune on account of love for God will be chosen to continue up the mountain. Only those chosen can make it to the top there to meet up with Christ on the summit. It is at the top of the mountain that the congregation of the just perfected in the way of Christ who constitute the true and living church is found.

Chapter Highlights

- ✓ The path of righteousness is a long and winding path ordained for those that obey God's will.
- ✓ The path that the righteous before God take is the road that leads to life where a few are found.
- ✓ It is by dutiful answer to God's call that Christ is realized to be duly manifested in the faithful.
- ✓ The Holy Ghost affirms spiritual transformation as the medium that God uses to communicate in light.
- ✓ Every believer will pass through a transitional period when he pauses before the door of destiny.
- ✓ It is baptism in the fire of the spirit of Truth that separates the eternal from the earthly.
- ✓ Lack of spiritual meat brings an uncertainty that robs the believer of peace and blessed assurance.
- ✓ The faithful fortified with spiritual meat will be empowered to change his surroundings for better.
- ✓ God uses the spiritual nighttime to teach and prepare the willing for the task ordained ahead.
- ✓ The believer is changed for better within when he labors to change others for good through love.
- ✓ Those who choose fame and fortune first will never make it to the summit of God's mountain.
- ✓ The combination of the Holy Ghost and Holy Spirit makes it possible to do all things through Christ.
- ✓ The congregation of the living church of Christ gathers at the summit of God's mountain.

The journey of faith ends on the distant hill

In greater love and light that counts no costs

But the faithful carries his burden up there

So as to leave the earthy and gain the starry

Chapter 5

THE NOBLE FISHERMAN

The believer that has received the gift of the Holy Ghost is able to know all things for he is privy to conversations in heavenly places. The dual combination of information availed by the Holy Ghost and power afforded by the Holy Spirit help to make all things possible. Both are availed to the faithful believer that has matured to join up in spirit with Christ Jesus as well as the other sons. Such is no longer a seeker after Christ but has found him to join the congregation of those living in divine light. The members of that elect body can know all that Christ Jesus knows and can do as he did in same light. This congregation is that of the mighty before God called to do the amazing through Christ. Therefore the faithful believer that has been received into this congregation is expected to do great and mighty things in God's name through Christ as one who has been availed great vision and strong faith.

The believer that has not yet come to spiritual maturity will lack the preparation and fortitude needed to take and occupy new grounds for Christ. Unless the believer is fully matured, there will be occasions in his life when he will be distracted by the voice of the prince of this world. This misleading voice ridicules the work of the kingdom of God as a waste of time while holding out the false promise of fame and fortune by the quick way. It seeks to beguile the unwary believer with enticements of 'you can have it now' that leads to spiritual death. It is all aimed at forestalling the spread of the kingdom of God by deceiving the unwary to labor for self instead of for the goodness of all.

The fast and broad way which many follow is the path of the self with little care about others. It promises quick rewards but never fulfills same. In contrast, the light of Christ guides the believer from darkness into a spiritual dawn through the righteous path. All believers who heed the voice of Christ to follow this path after his light will never be lost. They will be led on to the upward bound way towards the heavenly Father and to man's true home above. Such do escape the world to mount up with wings of the eagle to the mountain top of faith where the faithful come to be christened as sons of God in the light of Truth.

There are three things that are always attributable to those christened in true light. They bring fire, broiled fish and lay out bread. The fire that they bring is spiritual enlightenment, the broiled fish is a spirit transformed by faithful obedience to Truth and the bread is the word of God. In the last chapter of the gospel of John, Christ appears on the lakeshore bearing bread and broiling fish in fire. The fish represent those who were once lost but have been rescued from the dark sea of the world by Truth through the teachings of Christ. The spirit within is awakened to life to grow to maturity by faithful obedience to the words of Truth where received in good faith. It is by faithful obedience to Truth that the seeker is broiled in the fire of the spirit of life to become the transformed who finds true self in due season. Such that are broiled become the embodiment of Truth by which the 'blind' are able to see, the 'lame' walk and the bound in spirit freed. As the broiled in spirit faithfully share the word of Truth with the willing, greater understanding is availed for both sharer and receiver. Indeed as Truth is shared, divine light shines brighter so that more of Heaven's gifts can be received.

It is necessary for every follower after Christ to pass and endure baptism in the fire of Truth for without it none can meet up to be joined with him in spirit. Baptism in the fire of Truth avails the spirit of life but it asks of the believer to give his best to serve God in love. He may have to abandon fame, fortune and lose his old life as necessary for love of God in order to realize baptism in new life. It is the foundation of faith that he that dies in his old self for the sake of Christ will rise again with him in new life. To be willing to lose one's life or place in the world for love of God affirms true faith and is the hallmark of the righteous.

Broiling or spiritual baptism in the fire of Truth is the rite of passage that leads the faithful follower after Christ into full spiritual maturity. Spiritual baptism in the fire of Truth leads through the heart of the cross to rend the veil that separates the heavenly and earthly for the seeker. They that are fully matured in Christ can offer up sacrifices that will be well received by God. Such do not perform deeds for the praise of men but rather to please the heavenly Father as vessels well prepared to serve in light and love. The works that they are led in spirit to do are such by which God sheds his glory on mankind. The works of glory are certain assignments ordained from the foundation of the world for certain people to do on earth. Some who have been chosen to do such mighty works by God do not yet know it. And so, they must be duly awakened to realize who they are in God through Christ. The desire to serve God gloriously is a universal urge and drives the truly faithful to strive to remake earth in the order of Heaven.

The word of Truth is indeed the bread of life that must be shared with others through the teachings of Christ. Where truly desired and well received, the bread of life will turn into the meat of the spirit. It is the meat of the spirit that sustains the believer in his walk of faith. The believer must remain on the righteous path as Truth guides him in his walk for he cannot meet up with Christ unless he stays that course. He must continue to feed and live by the words of Truth if he is to be tuned in spirit to know God's will. Every seeker that is matured in Christ is given to know the will of God and will do as the heavenly Father wishes him to. Every son that lives his life as the Father wishes lives in the likeness of his father. The mystery of spiritual transformation is that everyone reborn in divine light is a son that lives with the mind and in image of the Father.

The believer that has grown into full maturity has passed through the heart of the cross to be transformed into the spiritual image of Christ Jesus. He is not a counterfeit for he has been minted from the original plate of the first born son of God. All who appear in the image of Christ are also given to walk in the power that it confers. The power availed to mankind through the cross of Christ must never be set to naught for it can move Heaven to action and earth to yield. The cross is the most exalted crucible for spiritual transformation available to mankind by divine will. In order for mankind to be connected to the heavenly Father, he must pass through the crucible that the cross represents. It must be that way if the flesh is to be rendered powerless and cease from inhibiting the spirit. Each believer must be able to bear his cross with due grace if he is to come into full spiritual maturity to be received as a son of God in divine light. It is through the burden of the cross that the faithful find spiritual release to commune with the Divine and join the heavenly household.

Providence frames God's tendency to intervene in earthly affairs to display his goodness and goodwill towards mankind. The scriptures refer to this tendency or domain as Zion. It is the source from which streams all of God's blessings received by mankind. Only the noble hearted who have answered God's call in faithful duty and to his delight find ready welcome into the domain of Providence. These are the faithful whose confessions of love for God and their fellow men are proven in light. Such are those that labor selflessly through Christ to rescue the lost out of the darkness of the world and to show them the way that leads to new life. Only such that labor selflessly in this light are worthy of the calling of Christ to be availed that which Providence brings forth. Only those that labor selflessly in love are duly changed in spirit through Christ from fishermen who take life to fishers of men who give life.

The things concerning God cannot be fully understood unless the believer is conditioned in spirit to receive them. The seeker must never be starved in spirit or true light will elude him. Many who follow after Christ often misunderstand the message because they are beclouded by the intrusions of a noisy world. They misunderstand due to an undernourishment of spirit that is borne from the compromise of Truth. As a result, they are not finely tuned to hear the Divine. They fail to comprehend because they lack the aid of the Holy Ghost to wisely inform them and help make things plain. Acting without knowledge of God's will often leads mankind to rely on own understanding and ill-judgment which often leads back to the old that should be left behind. God is always opening new veins of divine wisdom to be mined and new avenues of knowledge to be explored. He that is not tuned in spirit will miss out on the new things that God has planned for the season. The Spirit of Christ is the same yesterday, today and forever. The essence of Christ is the same and comes to maturity among all peoples and cultures of the world where God has so purposed. The believer who has stored up nuggets of Truth in good faith in the treasure chest of his heart to live thereby will be changed in spirit to become like Christ in due season. He will become a clone of Christ Jesus and share his spiritual attributes. He will be bestowed with the mind of Christ which is a reflection of the mind of God. Such is the same Christ that shows up in all colors, shades and hues within humankind for the external look becomes inconsequential where the spirit within mankind has come to full maturity in Christ.

It takes the cross borne in the way following after Christ to set the flesh to naught so that the spirit can be freed to soar heavenward. All who are fully transformed through Christ can soar to the exalted realm in spirit. Such share a common passion for God with goodwill that hopes for all mankind to connect with the heavenly Father in good and timely order. The exalted realm is the congregation of the souls justified before him that serves God worthily on earth. To serve God worthily is to share the good news of his salvation plan and live with love in the heart for all. This is what love and duty calls every true believer to do. He that carries out this heavenly business on earth in good faith will be informed and guided from the heavenly realm.

Every believer has to faithfully walk on the righteous path in order to meet up and become one with Christ. The righteous path leads through the heart of Christ and up to the hill of crucifixion. It is the only way for the old self to die so that the new in likeness of spirit with Christ can rise from within. The believer that is willing to bear the cross to the end as faith calls him to do will have his old nature die and the new in Christ emerge from within. He that emerges from the carcass of the old self is Christ. He is same one that shows up in the faithful all over the earth in same mind and spirit. The cross is a replicator of Christ Jesus. The faithful believer that is willing to endure its bitterness and humiliation to pass through its heart will be remade in the image of the Divine. He will be adopted into the family of God as a son of light and be counted among those who collectively represent the seed of the goodness of humanity acceptable to be used to accomplish God's designs on earth.

The sons of light are the foundation for the new creation on earth where the reign of the Christ will last forever. These have been prepared by God and positioned all over the world. They have been planted by the heavenly Father to bring in the last harvest of those souls who have been chosen for salvation from the foundation of the world but who are still spiritually lost. The lost that have been earmarked for salvation will not follow any other but the sons of light. The sheep know the voice of the shepherd. The voice of Christ though heard in different languages remains the same in spirit. Its effect on every sheep of the flock that is heaven bound is the same regardless of language. The sons have been transformed in light and prepared thereby to rescue the lost. Those that have been earmarked for salvation will always identify with the voice of Christ. Rescue of the lost is the mission which the God has set aside for the sons to fulfill. The crest of Christ is the hallmark and rescuing of the lost the calling of every son.

Such is the voice of destiny that calls the faithful to the field of harvest. He that has been so called has no choice in the matter but to yield to the will of the heavenly Father. He has to leave the old life behind so that he can step fully into the new. In as much as the wool of the lamb of sacrifice covers mankind's sins, it takes the fisherman's cloak to affirm readiness to help in rescuing those lost in the world. He that has donned the fisherman's cloak no longer seeks after the glory of the world but after God's approval. For the faithful that dons the fisherman's cloak, there is no better fulfillment to be found than to help bring the lost into the light of Christ. For the fisherman, the true fish to be sought after are the erstwhile lost souls pre-destined for salvation but who do not it yet know.

The faithful called to carry out the mission of Christ must do all in his power to dwell in peace with all men in order to prove effective. He must dwell spiritually in the peace of Jerusalem so that he can afford to stand on the Holy mount to be availed great vision and strong faith. He that spiritually dwells in the peace of Jerusalem to stand on the Holy mount may be surrounded by turmoil but he will be unperturbed by such to have access to the blessings of Zion. It is peace never availed to those that profess to love Christ for what they can get in material benefits but rather for those that truly love God and the divine way.

The matured in Christ must never neglect to share what is divinely availed and received with the willing in love. The essence of Christ is to give of one's self for the benefit of humanity. Christ does not seek his own but the benefit of all. Christ will never be without for the Father loves him much and will grant him that which his heart desires. Therefore the matured in Christ lives in contentment based on this irrevocable assurance of the heavenly Father's love. He knows that he will always abound in the fullness of the riches of God. Some of these riches may be obvious but others may only be perceived in spirit by the pure of heart. Material benefits may come along in the way but it should never be the motivation to love Christ. Rather the desire of every true seeker should be spiritual transformation in the image of Christ through the light of Truth and love. Every true seeker must seek after spiritual transformation for it affords the needful in life but it is bestowed in accordance with the will of God.

Chapter Highlights

- ✓ The faithful received into the living congregation of Christ are given to do mighty works in God's name.
- ✓ The fast and broad way of the world promises quick rewards that are never fulfilled in the end.
- ✓ Every believer must pass through the broiling of the fire of Truth before he can meet up with Christ.
- ✓ The faithful that labors to share Truth in love will be blessed with spiritual gifts and divine wisdom.
- ✓ Baptism in spirit in the fire of Truth rends the veil that separates the heavenly from the earthly.
- ✓ The son that lives in accordance with his Father's wishes is duly transformed into his likeness.
- ✓ The power divinely availed to mankind through the cross can move Heaven to act and earth to yield.
- ✓ The true confessor before God cannot help but have love and compassion for his fellow man.
- ✓ The essence of Christ is universal and abounds fully wherever faithfully welcomed into the heart.
- ✓ The faithful that love Truth share a common passion for love of God and goodwill towards all.
- ✓ Harmony with the Divine affords unperturbed peace even when man is surrounded by turmoil.
- ✓ Some divine riches are obvious but others can only be perceived in spirit by the pure of heart.

The search for the eternal is through love

Tis never been about finishing first or last

But about living to make sure that no one

Deserving is left behind or lost in the way

Chapter 6

LIGHT FOR ALL

The Spirit of Christ is a communion of saintly spirits and his body a corporation of those willing to share life's gifts with others in loving grace. This commonwealth of spirits justified before God is governed by bye-laws that are written into the heart. Only those that love God with a pure heart and have been purified by Truth to be spiritually matured in Christ are to be found in this 'living church'. Such are the reborn in light that dwell in a court of holiness by sovereign will and heavenly mandate in accordance with laws that are higher than man's earthly ones. Only those who have embraced Truth and live selflessly for the benefit of humanity in love can realize full spiritual maturity in Christ to be called therein. It should also be well noted that no one is able to come to full spiritual maturity in Christ unless it is in accordance with God's will for his life.

The matured in Christ, as the reborn or christened in light, are the building blocks of the kingdom of God. Such are given to change man's earthly ways that displease God into the heavenly that pleases him. Although called from the beginning, their place in the divine order is only assured and sealed as they bring others into God's fold through Christ. No one can be 'christened' or reborn in divine light unless such have served to father others into the kingdom of light. The building blocks of the kingdom are the faithful that go as God sends and obey as he urges them in spirit. Only such can be ordained to model the true way so that true seekers can follow after them to realize spiritual maturity in the light of Christ. Only such can be tuned in spirit to be privy to conversations in heavenly places so as to be well-equipped to nurture both the young and the struggling in faith.

The building blocks of the kingdom of light are the collective spirits of the saintly that line the way to whisper words of soothing comfort to those who follow after them. It turns out to be timely and well needed encouragement tendered in love by those who have finished the race to those who are still on the way. And so the spirits of the saintly join up with the angelic hosts to convey the up-and-coming along the heavenly way. It takes such love rendered by the saintly to sustain the young in faith as well as maintain the heavenly highway so that it is ever filled with resounding joy that echoes to herald each soul won for Christ and every birth into the kingdom of light.

The up-and-coming in the way after Christ deserve every

encouragement and support for the enemy of God considers them to be easy picking. The journey of faith gets more wearisome as the seeker travels further along on the path of righteousness. It seems to get narrower, more confining and very foreboding. The seeker after Christ is often weary and seemingly alone. Yet there seems to be a long way still to go before he can get to the destined horizon. Such may weary in the flesh but get stronger in spirit with every step taken. Although he appears to be walking alone yet no true seeker after Christ is ever really alone. There are unseen throngs of the saintly perfected in Christ who line up the way to offer spiritual encouragement to all. Their encouragements of love evoke a spiritual breeze that urges every true seeker forward and fills him with hope. It is encouragement that helps to shorten the distance and compress time to a great extent. The trek may be very harrowing but it is that which must be completed for the seeker to be sealed with Christ.

The faithful that is sealed in or bonded with Christ has become a son of mercy. He is sealed in the bond of the everlasting love of God from which he can never be separated by anything either in Heaven or earth below. Every seeker must strive to finish the race when the prize is within sight. The prize is within sight when the saintly spirits who have already finished the race come to aid. They come to make sure that the up-and-coming in the way that has the prize of glory within sight finishes what is left of the race before him. The race for eternal life through the way of Christ is not about finishing ahead of everyone. Rather it is about finishing together and making sure that no one deserving is left behind. The saintly brother with wisdom fills up the brother that lacks through Christ. The saintly brother with vision gives sight to the blind that are without through Christ. The saintly with the 'legs' becomes the ambulance for the lame through Christ. It is only when the saintly has established that there is no one deserving stranded on the way that he considers the job finished. Only then has he completed the work divinely ordained for him from the foundation of time.

The importance of praying for the saints should never be under estimated. It is very helpful for every faithful believer to cultivate the habit of praying for those that have gone before him. It is like asking the help of the big brother who has been there and done that already. The saintly spirits walk in the light of Christ with exemplary distinction. Therefore they are very needful and useful in the work of the kingdom of God in helping the true seeker. It is the sacrifices of the saints, spiritual and otherwise, that make possible the completion of the journey for those who follow after them. Without their aid, most will give up and fail to meet up with Christ in their faith walk.

The saintly in spirit are not perfect for only God is but he has passed a certain threshold in the divine reckoning. The saintly soul is like gold tried and purified in the furnace of

Truth. An assay of one hundred percent for gold is not realistic or easily attainable for all intents and purposes. However a ninety percent assay is the minimum threshold for certification of gold as pure. Beyond that minimum is the next upper level of ninety-five percent assay which is the premium level of purity. Finally, there is the ninety-nine percent assay which is the highest and ultimate level of purity. These levels of purity mirror the degrees of confidence by which statistics determines certainty in every group in nature. It does not matter if the discussion is about apples, oranges or souls of men. The same Truth applies universally to all in nature mankind included. In effect, there is an unending perfecting process much like the purification of gold in which the faithful are enmeshed where the light as well as the glory is ever increasing.

Every man has the natural impulse to do what is right in his own eyes. Furthermore, mankind is reluctant to act unless it serves his self interest in some way or another. That is the core of humanity's problems for one man's perceived act of goodness is often seen by another as misguided. He that is hailed for an act of goodness today can be denounced tomorrow for the same act. The truth of the matter is that natural man cannot trust himself nor can he be trusted by others. He is a conformist easily carried about by any wind and will follow as the rest goes. In consequence, all of natural man's self-righteous actions are filthy rags in God's eyes and do not count for much as they mostly disrupt and negate his plans for mankind.

On the other hand, the spiritual man is guided and acts under the will of God. He does not act on self-impulse to please self or for men to praise him. He does not act because it is the convenient or conventional thing to do. He performs his acts of goodness according to a standard different from that of natural man. Because the spiritual man acts according to a set of standards laid out by God who can be trusted, he can as a result be trusted by others with some degree of certainty. Again whether with apples, oranges or men the same Truth applies. The range between ninety and one hundred percent define the region of perfecting where the seeker after Christ desires to be. It is the range where the matured in spirit through Christ are found and the arena where the saintly in spirit abound to God's glory.

Saintliness is not a matter of the flesh but of the spirit. Whether inhabiting a living body or not, the saintly in spirit is an eternal being. There is a common lack of spiritual sight among those who profess to follow after Christ for many are not able to perceive the saintly in their midst. Many fail to realize who God has elected to be the mediator in their midst and model the heavenly way for them. This failure results from the fact that many prefer to go by sight rather than by faith. The saintly are spiritually exalted beings that appear to be of a low degree in the eyes of the world in many instances but are much more than they seem to be. Therefore, they are overlooked rather than shown the reverence and appreciation that they deserve. They are very often marginalized to dwell on the edge of society. Even in their own homes and among their own communities they are denied their proper place of honor. Today's world would be a far different and much better place, if the saintly were duly honored. Every believer must learn to pray for spiritual sight so that he may come to know the saintly in his midst for such are not known by human eyes but perceived through the light of Christ. They are revealed by God to every true seeker through the eyes of the spirit.

Although the saintly are often found in the little place on the edge of society, yet they occupy the spiritual housetop as vehicles chosen by God to receive blessings on behalf of humanity. More importantly, they are used by God to speak about the things that displease him which men do and hide in their hearts. It is by way of this revealing light that many come to change their ways as they realize that nothing is hidden from God's sight. The housetop on which the saintly dwell in spirit is of much strategic importance in the work of God's kingdom. Only the saintly that dwell on the spiritual housetop can foresee coming dangers and shout out the warnings to any who will heed. Only those that dwell on the spiritual housetop can be used by God to bring in the last harvest of souls for it is only through the housetop that the means can be found to meet Christ when the room is full and the way is blocked.

The dwellers on the 'corner of the housetop' have been spiritually positioned to spy the believer that is stranded in the way. This is the believer who has not received the Holy Ghost and therefore is not able to hear from heavenly places. The stranded are mostly those that have presumed to love both God and the world at the same time. This is the believer who loves the way of the Christ but cannot let go of the world. Such a professed follower becomes stranded for he is unable to disconnect from the worldly sufficiently enough to allow the words of God to take root in his heart so that his spirit can fully abound to be tuned to the Holy Ghost. In contrast, the faithful believer that lets go of the world will have the words of God take root to where his spirit will abound in Christ to become privy to conversations in heavenly places.

The dwellers on the spiritual housetop are like trees of righteousness that have been pruned by God to produce even more good fruit. It is on account of this pruning which makes them to seem little in the eye of the world that the spiritually blind fail to perceive their true worth in God's kingdom. Unbeknown to the blind, God in his infinite wisdom has prepared them through lowliness of spirit to lead those willing to embrace Truth from the darkness of the world into redeeming light through Christ.

Chapter Highlights

- ✓ The saintly in spirit are purified of heart and live by a heavenly mandate in accordance with God's will.
- ✓ The believer's place in Christ is not assured unless he faithfully shares Truth with others in love.
- ✓ The highway to heaven is filled with joy that echoes to herald each new birth into God's kingdom.
- ✓ The walk after Christ gets more challenging as the faithful travels farther along on the righteous path.
- ✓ The quest for eternity is not about finishing first but making sure that none deserving is left behind.
- ✓ The saintly in spirit are not perfect but have passed a certain acceptable threshold in God's eye.
- ✓ Mankind's self-righteous acts count for little with God as they disrupt and negate his good plans.
- ✓ The spiritual man lives not self-righteously but is led along a divinely ordained path from above.
- ✓ The saintly in spirit may appear little in the eyes of the world but he is exalted in the eyes of God.
- ✓ The saintly in spirit are divine vehicles even though they may dwell in relative obscurity.
- ✓ The seeker who presumes to love both God and the world will be stranded along the way.

The matured in Christ is a master chef in life's kitchen

Who speaks the right words in certain circumstances

As ingredients well blended to cook up the delightful

In wisdom and insight to please the palate of the soul

Chapter 7

IN GREATER MEASURE

Many who profess to follow after Christ are only able to connect with two dimensions of the Divine. Such can only grow in spirit to become brides of Christ and no more. However a few who follow after him grow in spirit to connect with three dimensions of the divine essence. They spiritually grow from brides of Christ to become sons who come into communion as one with God. In that case, they are no longer just followers after Christ Jesus but have met up with him to become spiritual sons of the heavenly Father's divine household. Many are called to the mountain of God and make it two-thirds of the way up to a certain ledge but only a few are chosen to make it to the summit. The sons of God make it to the summit but the brides of Christ can only make it to the ledge. God who knows the heart and capacity of all men has made it so. Man has no choice in this matter for God is the final arbiter there. He knows who is willing to forsake all for his sake. He also knows who will forsake some but not all things. The heavenly Father is the potter and man is the clay. Be that as it may, God still uses the brides of Christ to great effect in the work of his kingdom of light.

There is the work of the greater enlightenment and then that of the lesser enlightenment in God's kingdom of light. Most of the work done on earth by those who follow after Christ are of the lesser enlightenment and serve to bear babies in the way of light. The brides of Christ are the sheep that bear the lamb or bring others to join the flock. That work is great and highly necessary but it is not carried out under greater enlightenment. Most seekers who follow after the footsteps of Christ end up as brides who can only carry out the work of lesser enlightenment. However a few do grow in spirit to become sons of God able to carry out the works of greater enlightenment.

Only the sons can be used by the heavenly Father to carry out the works of glory or greater enlightenment. The sons of God are the shepherds that can model the way for the few among the flock divinely appointed to reach full maturity in Christ. The sons have been ushered into the Father's presence to be bestowed with eternal life and so they only can bring the dead back to life or help lead the chosen to eternal life. Only to them will God entrust the deeper and eternal truths. Only to them will the heavenly light shine fully so that all can be known by them as due. Only to the sons of God are availed needed tools to break new ground, permanently change the spiritual landscape, and bring down strongholds of spiritual wickedness to recreate the earth in heavenly order. However the work of greater enlightenment cannot begin unless that of the lesser enlightenment has been laid down first.

The sons of God have been chosen from the foundation of the world as 'sacrificial lambs' that will follow in the same trail as Christ Jesus to join up with him as brethren in the heavenly father's abode. They have been chosen to go to that place close to the heart of God that most believers are not able to go. They are like the high priests of ancient Israel who were the only ones allowed behind the veil. They have been elected because it has pleased God to do so. As mentioned previously, the sons are connected to the three dimensions of the Divine but the brides only two. Those that are connected to three dimensions can do the glorious for only to them does God give great vision and strong faith. Only they can leaven the whole meal. Those that have two measures can do good work but are limited in what they can do. It is for this reason that Christ Jesus always choses the same three to go with him up to the summit for not all can go there. The rarified and purified height is only for the chosen few.

It is for this reason that there is a constant and repetitive reference in the Holy Scriptures about the 'twos' and 'threes' gathered together with Christ Jesus in their midst always. The reference is most often linked to quantity but it is really about capacity. The brides are the vessels of two firkins whereas the sons are the vessels of three firkins used for purification that turn water into sweet wine. It is for this reason that the prophet Isaiah speaks of two or three remaining fruits in the uppermost boughs of Israel. It is for this reason that Christ Jesus took only three out the twelve disciples to the mount of transfiguration. It is for this reason that only one out of the four soldiers who parted the garments of Christ Jesus received the seamless robe of immortality. Most that follow after Christ know only two dimensions of the divine nature and so never know the Father. Indeed such may be friends of Christ but not sons of God. They will never get to stand justified before God for they have not been chosen to do so.

The believers with spiritual capacity to connect to the two dimensions of the Trinity will continue to enjoy divine grace through Christ for that is the reward of their labor. They will not have immortality of soul for they have their portion in this world and fill their bellies with earthly treasure. They follow after Christ for gain and have chosen material rewards as their bliss. They have failed to be nurtured through grace on to mercy. Such that are stuck in grace often become constipated and that is the malaise of the earthly churches today. Such have marginalized those connected with the three dimensions of the Divine and accuse them of heresy. They have marginalized those willingly to forego fame and fortune for eternal habitation with the heavenly Father. They have marginalized those who have chosen to rule with Christ Jesus as sons of God in the kingdom of light. Though disparaged and reviled by the spiritually blind, the sons have become established in light and gather around close to the divine heart under mercy. They have walked on the path of righteousness as led by the Holy Spirit to become transformed in Divine likeness as immortal souls. It is for such that the inheritance of the new Heaven on earth waits as the best that has been saved for last.

Humanity has entered the season for the manifestation of the sons of God. The latter have been positioned over the world in all colors, cultures and tongues. All who seek to know and call on God sincerely will perceive the son in their midst. Many who profess to follow after Christ are stuck in the way due to not being well informed. They stagnate in the churches with walls where men often sing their own praises using God's name as prop. However it has been divinely appointed for some to grow out of that indolence of spirit into greater enlightenment. Only then will the stagnated in spirit come into full maturity in Christ and thereby find fulfillment within the Divine. Many who profess to follow after Christ lack this knowledge. They have to know the Truth about the separate callings of the brides and sons so that no one is denied his prize for the race is not the same for all. Every true believer must know so that he can faithfully finish the race set before him by God in order to receive his due reward.

Every son of God when perceived must be placed on the tallest of candle sticks so that others may come to 'see' better through him for he brings greater light. Every son is a catalyst to enable the stagnated in spirit grow into full spiritual maturity in Christ. God invests a lot in each son to remake them in the divine image for good reason. He nurtures and protects them through the jaws of death because the hope of redemption and salvation for their blind fellows rests with them. He has entrusted the sons with a message for humanity that could not be timelier or more needed now than ever before. The message is for humanity to come into the safety of Christ to join in fellowship with the divine Father and the sons. He that desires to join them must not worry about what everyone else is doing or what is going on in the world. His heart must be set on the things that bring glory to God. However he must be true to himself and listen to his heart so that he can respond to that which God asks of him. He must remain in the instant. He must take each step as the spirit within directs him moment by moment and day by day.

Victory through Christ is garnered in living by moment to moment and from glory to glory. There is so much to be gained even in the little when God is involved in it. The faithful believer must approach the heavenly Father always with good expectations. He must remain hopeful in all things and must never give up. He must never cease to call on God and to trust in the goodness of the Father who never forsakes his own. The believer must fill the lamp of his heart with the oil of God's words so that the light of Truth can continue to shield him from pervasive darkness in the world today. The psalms and spiritual songs serve to keep the faithful believer in the middle of faith's road so that he can finish the course that he has embarked on. It serves every faithful believer well to learn to sing the songs that testify to the goodness and unfailing faithfulness of God. He must allow God's praise to tune his voice for it is that which lifts man's soul above the trappings of the worldly to connect with the heavenly.

Everyone appointed for a place in the kingdom of God has a certain task ordained for him. Every believer must learn not to force the issue or people for that matter for everything in the kingdom of light is done in accordance with God's will. It takes his Holy Spirit to will and work through the faithful to accomplish divine purposes. The believer must remain assured that God who always has a glorious plan for the faithful will bring that which he has initiated to the best outcome in due season. Everyone received into the kingdom of light will be used to accomplish tasks that manifest divine power. Such is the power of God that it shows up through Christ in different peoples and places to carry out his divine will. It is the sons being used to do amazing works to bring glory to God today as in times past as well as in the future.

It is only when Christ has come to full spiritual maturity within the believer that all the words written in the tablet of the heart link together to form a harmonious whole. Only when that comes about will the life in the words spring forth to bring about the amazing from seemingly nothing. It mirrors the process by which the universe was 'called' into existence. It is that which creates new life through Christ. It is by such that the matured in Christ becomes a regenerator to induce life out of the dying and the new from the old. Such can break stones or bend metals to the desired shape with words in accordance with God's will. The words of God never passes away for therein is the foundation upon which all things rest. Truth when established in the believer's heart will never die but will always have life that springs forth at God's appointed time. It remains latent in the believer's heart until God brings around the due season for its glory to shine forth.

The faithful in whom Christ has come to full maturity must confess it for he has become a candle lit by God that no evil wind can blow out. Such is a source of light that must not be hid for it is a beacon to guide true seekers. Full maturity in Christ comes about for the believer when he is at his wit's end and the flesh is set to naught. It is only then when the flesh has yielded that the new man of the spirit within shows forth to lead the believer forward in mercy and on to the works of glory at God's behest. It is then that the day of glory dawns and the believer can begin to change the world for better in heavenly order.

Chapter Highlights

- ✓ The believer connected to three dimensions of the Divine has met up and walks in company of Christ.
- ✓ There is the work of the greater enlightenment as well as that of the lesser in the kingdom of God.
- ✓ The sons of God are the true shepherds who guide the sheep of the flock to full maturity in Christ.
- ✓ The sons are sacrificial lambs and spiritual brethren who follow the same time-worn trail as Jesus.
- ✓ Many that follow after Christ are only able to experience two dimensions of the divine Godhead.
- ✓ The spiritually blind often marginalize those that forego fame and fortune for eternity with God.
- ✓ Every believer must run and finish the race set before him by God for it is not the same for all.
- ✓ The sons of God are candles to be held up so that mankind can see in greater light by them.
- ✓ Only by filling the heart with the oil of Truth can the flame of Christ be shielded from evil winds.
- ✓ The believer must learn not to force the issue but trust God to make good things happen for him.
- ✓ The word of God never dies when established in heart but will spring forth to life on Heaven's cue.
- ✓ The spiritually matured in Christ is a candle lit with divine love that no evil wind can blow out.

Truth is the divine mirror by which each man

Comes to perceive and change self for better

In Truth lies the power that can free the spirit

And uplift mankind to star in heavenly places

Chapter 8

FREED BY TRUTH

There is great power in Truth to free and enable man's spirit to soar to the starry heights. Truth is the mirror by which each man comes to know and change self for better. Most men say that they would rather be told as well tell the truth. However and sadly, that is often not the case. The whole world seems to feed on lies in some form and to various degrees. Be that as it may, it is not part of man's nature to tell lies but an acquired habit. Mankind knows that to tell lies is not the right thing to do yet he cannot stop from doing so. In a way, mankind has become like the addict whose partaking of the little folly of life often turns into a monster that he cannot control.

Each time that man tells lies he loses a little bit of himself in the process. He de-grades both self and humanity as a whole when he does that. By telling lies he disrupts his divine connection and distances himself further from God. Lies negate godliness to set the divine to naught for God is Truth. The man that tells lies has allowed a virus to infect the essence of goodness within that defines humanity. He has made room for a foreign species to invade and take over the landscape of his mind. Lies do not sit right with most men. Lies discomfort and often make people squirm. Mankind tells lies in order to gain an advantage materially or otherwise. Such that have not seen the light justify the telling of lies on a risk and reward rationale. They reason that if no one is obviously hurt or if the resulting damage is minimal according to their estimation, then the reward justifies the means. The irony is that such gains turn out to be short-lived and regrettable. In the long run, lies leave traces of bitterness in the victim and a blotch on the soul of the perpetrator. Lies are not worth the trouble for they engender mistrust and leave a sour after-taste in the mouth. Truth on the other hand may be bitter initially but it invariably leaves a sweet after-taste in the mouth after all is said and done.

The word of God is the ultimate Truth which abides to never pass away. He in whose heart the word of God has found a welcome home will duly come to full spiritual maturity in Christ. He will abide forever even as the words within him do to become an eternal vessel meet for the service of God. He will become that tree planted beside still waters whose leaves remain verdant and evergreen. The leaves that the tree bears are words spoken from the heart to bring healing to anyone who will receive them in good faith. He that speaks healing words has become a fountain of divine wisdom and the wellspring of life as well as an immortal soul whose consciousness will ever be.

The immortal souls are such that have become sons of the heavenly Father through Christ. They have been planted and established by God all over the world. Their lines of communication do show forth for their branches have gone all over the world spiritually. They are the brethren of Christ Jesus and are linked up in a world wide web of life that derives its consciousness from God's heavenly throne above. They are heard and understood by all whose hearts hunger after righteousness and seek after the knowledge of God in Truth.

The message of Christ Jesus has reached every corner of the world and been adequately preached to all. The stage has been set as mankind enters into the season of final harvest where the flesh matters but little but the spirit counts for most. Mankind has neither found satisfaction with promotion of self nor relief in his excessive gouging of the flesh. He keeps looking for ways to bend God's rules where he has not done so already in his headlong rush into degeneracy. In consequence, he feels even emptier in his core with each passing day as he realizes that the flesh has become spent in its offerings and no longer satisfies as in times past for it has nothing new or meaningful to offer. Such offerings that many lusted after in times past much like stale wine have just about run its course. But for the believer who has received the word of Truth, it is a season of new life and re-awakening in divine light.

All in whom the words of God did not take root to grow

and produce good fruit have no place in the new age about to unfold. The new age is for the bearers of pitchers of living water and those deemed righteous by God. In the unfolding new age, the collective spirit embodied in the sons of light will control and determine the course of events in accordance with divine will. The heavenly Father has imputed his righteousness into the sons and bestowed them with the mind of Christ so that they may know his will. It is in this way that the sons come to inherit the earth as God exercises his will on earth through them.

The sons of light are the faithful in Christ and have been prepared by God for this season. Such are the lone trees who have produced good fruit and have been pruned by God to produce even more. It will become a great dawn for humanity as the season reaches full bloom and God sheds more of his glory on the sons. In the prelude to the season of great dawn each son must remain true to his calling so that the fruit he produces will be shielded from corruption by the enemy. They have been prepared and set apart by God and must remain dedicated to serve in a special way. They have sacrificed much in the short-term in order to undergo spiritual transformation and obtain the priceless in the long term. They have been willing to embrace Truth and follow in the light after Christ Jesus and are not embarrassed to declare him as Lord before all. The sons of light have duly become exalted in spirit as well as depositories of the sacred and hidden divinely revealed by which the everlasting is founded.

Spiritual transformation in divine image or christening in the light of God's truth is the rite of knighthood through the way of peace as modeled by Christ Jesus. During this passage in which the old self and its debased nature dies, a new remade in the image of Christ comes to life. The new man of Christ within is stirred to life, nourished to maturity and called forth at God's bidding. It is akin to the 'death of Lazarus' so that a new man can be called forth to life to dine and eat meat with Christ. The fully transformed in spirit or christened in divine light has been planted in the fountain of life which is God himself to be nourished there with the meat of Truth. The meat is that which is hidden in plain sight to most but revealed to those who have died in the old self and re-awakened in the new of Christ. Because the sons have been pruned by God to produce even more good fruits, they often seem little in the eyes of the world. However they are duly revealed soon enough on Heaven's cue to the true seeker for who they are and what they bring through Christ in accordance with God's will.

The sons are remade in divine image and revealed in light in the same way as the burial swaddles of Lazarus are unwrapped. They are revealed to those that seek in Truth to receive in love and good hope. They are ushered forth by the heavenly Father as the knights of Christ who wield the sword of the Divine. The sword that they wield is knowledge and wisdom divinely availed by eating meat in the company of Christ Jesus. They gather around the mercy seat of the throne of God as those borne of strong faith but are ushered forth into the world as sons of mercy. They are sons of mercy for they hold the hope of clemency and new beginning for seekers that embrace Truth by them. The world is about to change as the lines which separate the godly and ungodly among mankind, which have been blurred hitherto, is coming into sharp focus. Soon all things will be revealed for what they really are and where they belong in creation.

There is really no other way or short-cut to gain entrance into the congregation of the sons of light than through Christ Jesus for he is the door. The seeker after true light must begin by embracing the word of Truth, staying faithful to it and sharing same with others. As one lives by Truth, the spirit of new life in Christ will be awakened within him. And as he continues to feed on the word of Truth in faithfulness and sincerity, the spirit of life that has come alive within him will continue to grow as well. Meanwhile as the new within continues to mature in this new light, the old nature will steadily die off. It is by this displacement or transformation of the debased old into the purified new that Christ comes to full maturity within. The new life that awakens to grow to full maturity within the faithful believer is a spiritual clone of Christ Jesus and in communion with God. Such is one whose spirit has become well commended to God. Man's spirit is at its loftiest, his mind at its purest and his heart at its noblest when in communion with the divine Father. He who has been fully transformed in spirit through Christ will be imputed with righteousness so that all his actions will reflect the will of the Father. Much in the mold of Christ Jesus, all who have been fully transformed in this light are equipped to do the works that bring God due glory but with more tools available to him today than in the past.

Every son of light is linked up worldwide with all the others that God has planted all over the world. Each one is a node or an outlet for divine impetus positioned in the world to serve the cause of goodness in accordance with God's will. Though all the sons are sundered afar, they are connected in spirit in a web of life with the mercy seat of God at the hub. It is a web connected in Truth that pulses with divine consciousness and in love as the fountain of the everlasting that endures to fulfill. The sons of light labor together subconsciously to rally in spirit to each other's aid as they serve God's will on earth. Theirs' is a spiritual relationship of a very high order that God uses to do the marvelous on earth and to shed his glory on mankind. Having been transformed in divine light to be God's proxies among mankind, the sons have also been duly entrusted with much to their care. For that reason, they need not live out the rest of their lives on earth as mere mortals but as those endued with great power and minds sharpened to change the world in accordance with God's will in the present as well as for all ages to come.

The words of scriptures are not all understood in a moment of time. They are progressively revealed over the passage of time as the believer faithfully seeks for better understanding. There are some truths that can never be understood until the season divinely appointed for them dawns. Such are like seeds that require soaking in a good amount of water before they can germinate. There is a morning appointed for each hidden truth and that day must dawn before its fullness can be duly understood. However mankind has entered into the last days of this age and consequently much of the truths 'hidden' within the scriptures have come to be understood in good measure. The 'hidden' make up the meat of the word that only the matured in Christ can understand as the key to the mysteries of God's kingdom and fullness of his riches.

The riches and glory of God can only be realized through a full measure of the meat of the spirit that comes from obedience to Truth. He that ministers God's words to others but has no knowledge of God's hidden truths is a bride of Christ. Such is not able to eat the meat of the word or be privy to hidden truths. But he that ministers God's words to others and also has knowledge of the sacred hidden to most has progressed from the bride of Christ to become a son of God. He can eat the meat of the word and be privy to the sacred. The fullness of divine riches is reserved for the latter as sons of the new age bestowed with the mind of Christ to re-create the earth in the order of Heaven as in Eden past.

Chapter Highlights

- ✓ Truth is the mirror by which each man comes to know and change self as well as others for better.
- ✓ The man that revels in lies unwittingly disrupts the divine connection and estranges himself from God.
- ✓ The fully matured in Christ has joined up with the wellspring of life to become an immortal soul.
- ✓ The sons of God are heard and understood by all whose hearts are committed to seek after Truth.
- ✓ The unfolding age is for bearers of living water who render faithful service through Christ.
- ✓ The chosen of God are the strong of faith who through love become depositories of the sacred.
- ✓ The new man within is stirred to life, nourished to maturity and called forth duly at God's bidding.
- ✓ The elect are the sons of mercy who hold the hope for clemency and a new beginning for all believers.
- ✓ The Spirit of man that is commended to God has been lifted to its loftiest, purest and noblest.
- ✓ Every son is a divine node positioned to serve the cause of goodness in accordance with God's will.
- ✓ The words of scripture are not all understood in a moment but are progressively revealed over time.
- ✓ The follower after Christ that can eat the meat of the word will be privy to the sacred and hidden.
- ✓ The fullness of his riches is reserved for last by God for those who will inherit the earth.

The best is reserved for those who keep faith

Ones whose eyes always rest on God in hope

Who tarry to finish life's race in light as called

Through patient love that evokes the divine

Chapter 9

NEW WINE FOR NEW VESSELS

In the divine dispensation the new sweet wine that has never been tasted before is served at the end of the marriage feast contrary to the world's way. It is served when most have been filled with the less to the few who tarry in good hope. Only those who tarried to complete the journey of spiritual transformation can receive the new wine reserved for last. Only those who have waited to be covered with the new cloth of eternity with the Divine which never waxes old can hold the new wine. The fullness of the riches of God is reserved for the immortal souls that have been commended to God. It is served to those who have been willing to yield to God to be woven into the web of eternity through Christ. To be woven into eternity is the crown of faith and an experience ordained for the noble hearted few that truly love God and humanity.

He that is willing to love God above all through Christ will come to be entrusted with those things upon which Heaven and earth are founded. He will be joined up with kindred spirits that find joy and fulfillment in carrying out as the Divine urges in love. He that has become a vessel filled with divine gifts must always share with the needy in love for it is in so doing that they come to be refilled with more and better through Christ.

The most important gift of all to be shared through Christ is the message of redemption and hope of eternity. Not many embrace that message but the few who do come to experience joy and fulfillment of soul availed in love from the heavenly Father above to men below. Only those redeemed from darkness into the light of Christ are ever freed in spirit to experience true joy and fulfillment. Man can only find joy and fulfillment when the comforter is availed to him. The comforter is the Holy Ghost and the medium by which the veiled is communicated from the mercy seat of the Father to the faithful. He is the medium by which the Father affirms the faithful believer on earth. The Holy Ghost is he that bears information from heavenly places so that the faithful below can be endued with hidden knowledge and wisdom as needed. 'He' brings information from heavenly places in timely order in the due moment and dawning season.

God chooses and keeps vessels apart in order to avail them spiritual gifts such as the Holy Ghost to share with others in love. Such vessels receive the desires of their heart because they know what to ask for by the Holy Ghost informing them about what to ask for. It is in this light that they have pre-knowledge of what to ask for as well as when to intercede by prayer on behalf of others. And so, every chosen vessel offers up sacrifices as well as receive God's blessings for the benefit of all. It is a mission carried out in love that continues until God wills otherwise for the things concerning Christ end for the faithless.

Many who confess his name and preach the message of Christ Jesus use his words to promote self and other agenda. Christ will never come to full spiritual maturity where there is abuse of grace and profaning of his name. They that do so can never be connected to the three dimensions of the Divine. They may have some measure of the spirit and of the word of Christ but they will never have knowledge of the Father. The believer connected to the three dimensions of the Divine has been brought by Jesus into the Father's presence. He whom Christ Jesus has brought into the Father becomes a son even as he himself is. He that has been brought to meet the Father will awake in his divine likeness. Only those who have come into the Father can truly declare that Christ is alive. Only then is the believer availed the passport of eternal life that makes fulfillment or 'satisfaction' possible on earth.

He that has awakened in the likeness of the Father must declare Christ to be alive for the latter has come to full maturity within him. He that comes to full maturity within is the same Christ for he has been molded similarly in spirit as the first born son Christ Jesus. To declare Christ to be alive often sounds dubious in the ears to invite derision from many in the world and a charge of blasphemy from the spiritually indolent. For this reason, only the few who have borne Christ to full life within will dare declare him to have come alive. He is first seen with the eye of the spirit by those appointed to receive as he descends from the heavenly realm above to the earthly below. That first seen is the seed of the divine injected into the heart of the seeker so that the spirit within can be sparked to life.

'He' that descends from the heavenly to the earthly realm is the seed of promise of Christ. It is this seed planted in the believer's heart that takes at least seventeen years of faithfulness in the light of Truth and service to God to be nurtured to full maturity. It is this seed of promise grown to full term in the faithful believer that is declared to be Christ reappeared. The faithful in whom Christ has come to full maturity does not so much declare it by word of mouth as model it by his lifestyle, choices and actions. God will reveal Christ wherever he has come to full life and will be duly perceived wherever he has come forth. It is all in accordance with God's will for it is his anointing that brings Christ to full life within the chosen as well as open men's eyes to perceive where same has come forth to full life.

God's throne is established in mercy but the sons can only be commended in spirit with the Father through grace. The heavenly Father grants his tender gifts to his sons in mercy who receive from him with due thanks to share with those that embrace Truth in grace. Often times the sons are despitefully used by men. They are counted as fools by the ignorant who presume to take the kindness of Christ for nothing. Sadly such do not know that it is folly to misuse, withhold or take grace for naught. However the true sons never count costs or dwell on hurt but continue rather in diligent service. They never cease from extending grace and sharing with others in love for they know that the flow of grace is ceaseless and divine gifts boundless for all who walk in sincere humility. They know that it will remain so until God decrees otherwise for the things concerning Christ end for the faithless.

The heavenly Father loves the sons because they love Christ Jesus. It is not possible to come to full spiritual maturity in Christ without God's commendation. As previously discussed, the journey to full spiritual maturity is a climb to the top of God's mountain. It is to the top of the mountain that one must ascend in order to escape the world. It is a journey that is costly in many ways but crowns the seeker with eternal life as well as access to the fullness of the riches of God. No one can make it to the top of God's mountain unless he is willing to embrace Truth regardless of cost or hurt to self. No one can make it to the summit on his own unless it has been ordained for him as it requires the divine wind to lift the seeker up there.

God's promise is to take care of the faithful that makes it to the top of his mountain. Such are the christened in light and his beloved ones that he has sworn to never leave or forsake. They have given all in the way to come into the Father's eternal habitation where the congregants dwell as one in spirit. The top of the mountain is Heaven's tableland where God prepares a place for the faithful in the presence of their enemies. It is the prize attained after all odds have been overcome. The believer that has faithfully embraced Truth to reach the top of the mountain has passed through the darkening veil of the earthly to be borne into the kingdom of God where all things glow. All things glow therein because they have been infused with the essence of the pure and true. All things glow therein because they have been purified in Truth and in love. All things glow therein because they have been touched by the caressing hand of the Divine.

The heavenly Father remains unseen but his glory reflects on all those that he draws close to himself. The place close to the heart of God is devoid of any darkness. The sons who have come into the Father no longer walk in darkness but in the full light of Truth. Their righteousness show forth for light surrounds them due to the angels that attend them. They walk on earth as points of light in a dark world speaking Truth in which they have been embalmed. It is this embalmment in Truth that protects them from the evil in the world and sets them apart for use by God.

The faithful that live and walk in the light of Truth are heaven bound sojourners given to pass through the earth as ghosts. They make indelible marks on earth and leave a trail of enlightenment wherever they have been. They are really sons of Heaven who make cameo and brief appearances on earth. He that has been commended with God in spirit will have the magnetism of the Divine induced in him. And by extension, all who have been induced with the divine magnetism will have the ability to draw other men to God. The magnetizing impulse is the love of God expressed in the spirit of Christ to draw all towards the Father of all and source of creation. It is impulse strongly felt by the believer and less so by the doubter.

All who come to duly know the sons and the Father are spiritual kindred who were foreknown from the foundation of time. In effect, the willing and believing are being led back to the home that they once knew in their distant past. It is for this reason that the sheep of the Father's flock know the voice of the sons of God. It is the same spirit of Christ which spoke through others in the past that speaks through them today and will continue to do so for ages to come. The matured in Christ speak not for themselves but for the benefit of lost mankind. Having been magnetized towards God, they desire nothing else but to help others experience the reality of God.

Within the divine fold of Christ can be found answers to the bedeviling in life. Therein mankind can be freed in spirit from all that ails him in the light of Truth. He will be able to find the joy and fulfillment that has eluded him. The words spoken by the sons are anointed by God for they are his oracles on earth. The sons give voice to words that come from the heavenly throne and are heard with the ear of the spirit by those appointed to receive same. They speak words that do not return void but accomplish intended objectives. Such are timely words of knowledge used to address matters at hand and issues of the day.

Many that profess to walk in light after Christ Jesus lack the power of the anointing of God. It cannot be bought or obtained in any other way except by Truth and spiritual maturity in Christ. Divine gifts cannot be afforded by fame, fortune or high regard in the world as God is no respecter of persons. The anointing of God though it is given freely is not free for man to use as he desires. It is given by God who searches the hearts and knows the intentions of men. The divine anointing is only for those who live not for self but for all. It is divinely availed to the noble hearted who live to serve God as well as humanity in Truth and love. The way of Christ is to seek the welfare of humanity and not just one's own. The faithful that live in that light will be blessed in many ways by God.

The power and benefits of Christ are appointed for those who live for all and love Truth as well. The blood of the lamb of sacrifice works only for those who live by Truth. The way that leads back to the heavenly Father is appointed for those that love Truth. Truth is the bond that joins all of God's own together. It is the cord of life that binds the worthy and faithful with the Father in eternity.

The scripture makes it clear that mankind can never find redemption from sin or salvation of soul except through a blood sacrifice. It further instructs that Christ Jesus is the Lamb of God chosen for that purpose from the foundation of the world. The power in the blood of sacrifice shed for mankind's sins can be appropriated when the seeker rejects the world's way to embrace God's through Christ. It is power that can only be appropriated by embracing Truth through Christ regardless of cost. Indeed it is costly to embrace Truth to live in the light of Christ but redemption and salvation far outweighs that in the end.

He that compromises Truth is a stranger to God who will not experience divine power. But he that loves Truth will be loved by God to experience divine power. The world hates the lover of Truth initially but comes to love him later. The world defames the truthful but praises him later. The world curses the truthful but blesses him later. The choice to follow after Christ is not for the faint hearted but for the brave of heart. Truth has the power to make the faint hearted brave. Such is the potency of the power of Truth that the lamb will bed down with the lion without fear. He that loves Truth must be willing to lose much in the world but he must trust God to make provisions to enable him live a victorious and fulfilling life regardless.

The believer that seeks after Christ must first turn his back on the way of the world for it is a dark path. He who walks in darkness can never meet up with Christ or experience the knowledge or power of God. The believer can live in the world but he need not be of it. The world pretends not to but it loves lies and pretends not to but it hates Truth. The soul that hates Truth is severed from the power in the blood of Christ. Mankind cannot love both God's way and the world's for there are opposites. He must choose either one or the other. The love of God leads to life everlasting whereas the love of the world leads to spiritual death.

The world is at the end of its course. Therefore to remain on that course is an unwise and losing choice. It is wiser to seek after God for the time is limited. The seeker who is on the way must not be discouraged if abandoned by the world for there must be a separation between the darkness and light before Christ can mature within. The mind must be free of the world so as to be full of hope for no one that serves two masters can know the Father. Although the seeker after true light may seem to be alone and despised, yet he never walks alone for Christ is with him always. He can only know this for sure in the darkest hours of life when he is separated from the world and all seems to be arrayed against him. It is only when he has walked through the valley of the shadow of death that Christ comes to full life within him. It is only then that all his fears will cease to be replaced by hope and love. Only then can he be a vessel of honor kept apart by God to render noble service for all to witness in glorious light.

Chapter Highlights

- ✓ The precious things of heaven are only entrusted to the selfless willing to forsake all for the love of God.
- ✓ The Holy Ghost is the medium by which the Father affirms and communicates with his sons.
- ✓ The sons know what to ask for from God because they are pre-informed by the Holy Ghost.
- ✓ He in whom Christ has come to full maturity shows it by his words and actions.
- ✓ Spiritual transformation and escape from the world is realized in the climb up God's mountain.
- ✓ Heaven's tableland is where God has prepared a place for the faithful to dine in wisdom and Truth.
- ✓ All who are drawn to Christ are spiritual kindred foreknown by God from the foundation of time.
- ✓ Words of Truth impart knowledge that addresses the matters at hand and the issues of the day.
- ✓ The anointing of God is given freely but only for the noble hearted who serve him in love and truth.
- ✓ Truth is the bond that joins all living things and leads the faithful back to the heavenly Father.
- ✓ It takes Truth and love to embolden the lamb to bed down with the lion without fear.
- ✓ God is always near for the faithful believer that loves Truth but very far for the soul that hates it.
- ✓ The vessels of honor are kept apart to render noble service for all to witness in glorious light.

The dark seasons repeat

As night follows the day

Serves to let man know

He is but little 'fore God

Chapter 10

VESSELS SET APART

The faithful in whom Christ has come to full maturity and revealed is a vessel set apart to be used mightily by God. He is one destined to do the marvelous before men that brings glory to God. God wills and does great things through such vessels to display his power on earth before mankind. The vessel so revealed must maintain a certain holiness and sobriety so as to remain ready to be used by God always. He is to remain ready by keeping the flame of Christ burning brightly in the heart by obedience to Truth and sharing life's gifts with all in love. Nothing else will serve mankind better in life than to observe God's commandments as revealed to him in the light of Christ.

There is no point in gaining the whole world but losing one's soul therein. There is also no point in having the likeliness of Christ and not having the anointing it avails. The chosen vessel must always be willing to pay the price or deny self as urged in spirit in the light of Truth and love so as to keep his soul and remain connected to the Divine.

He must not be offended or be bitter when the spiritually blind despise him for they reject not him but Christ (the embodiment of Truth) that he bears within. To live by Truth in the light of Christ and yet be free of bitterness in the heart is the only way to be spiritually connected as well as abound in divine anointing.

He that does not live Truth will hate those that do. The teaching of Christ Jesus is God's Truth availed in love to mankind. Sadly the untruthful will not be able to embrace Christ or come to know the Divine. But he that is able to receive Christ in good faith will duly mature in spirit to be in communion with the Divine. He that communes with the Divine will embody Truth and be given to speak as an oracle of God. Such will be hated by those who have rejected Truth even though that spoken forth is for the welfare of all. The rejection of Truth leads mankind into wicked ways and encourages the encroachment of darkness everywhere. Many in today's world reject Truth to live by hook and crook as it seems to have become an acceptable way to get ahead these days. Consequently, those who choose to live by Truth now look like proverbial fish out of water that are seen as peculiarly strange in the world. The world may be against the lovers of Truth but such must take heart in the knowledge that such hatred bears testimony to the presence of Christ within.

Those who live by Truth always have the angels of the presence of God near to watch over them. They may be few in number but they are in the majority for the power God is always at hand for them. Truth sanctifies and seals the faithful in a bond of love with God. The enemy may have a few prevailing moments against the truthful but such soon pass away. The truthful can afford victory in life for God's unseen hand always engages the enemy on their behalf to bring them due victory. It is for the lover of Truth that victory through the spirit of the living God has been ordained. Such must go forward in light to overcome and claim that which God has promised in love through Christ.

The faithful in Christ love Truth and therefore God who is Truth cannot stop from loving them. The bond of love that seals the Father and the faithful cannot be broken. The faithful may appear little in the eye of the world but they are the mighty in spirit given to produce good fruits abundantly. The 'little ones' in the world are dear to the heavenly Father above who will not deny their wishes. Indeed little is much when God is in it. The power of God shows forth mightily when the faithful appear to be weak and helpless. It is when the immeasurable love and tender mercies of the Father alight on his beloved. The faithful must therefore learn to listen at his weakest moments for help has been promised by the Father and is very near. The faithful must keep the trust in his most miserable moments and must hold on at the darkest hours. The power and love of the Father is fully manifested in the moments of trial. The still small voice of hope is heard loudest and the hand of God most visible in the moments of despair. This is when God does the marvelous for it is within the crucible of trial that the amazing is forged.

The faithful are called to hope and wish for those things that are true, honest, pure, just, lovely, of a good report and virtuous. Such wishes are realized when the words of Truth are written in the heart where the noise of the world will not becloud them, shielded and duly kept as should. The noise of the world dims the soul and smothers the flame of love within the heart. The things that man think about will take shape in his life for as the heart wishes so a man becomes. The mind that is not cluttered with wants leaves enough room for the needful to abound. But the mind that has been cleared of life's unwanted debris is freed from the cloudiness that inhibits great vision.

In the absence of cloudiness comes clarity so that all things can be seen clearly, known for what they are and where they should belong. There is no confusion as to which things are good or bad when the light of Christ governs life's choices. The faithful know that the good belong in the treasure chest of the near and dear while the bad on the other hand should be relegated to the dust bin of the distant and useless. When orderliness returns in life, his focus is sharpened so that mankind is no longer carried about by the opinion of others. Rather his spirit now free of clutter can soar to the exalted realm to be mightily blessed for there is no longer wanting, hasting or wasting when order governs life through the light of Christ.

The heavenly Father will make accommodation for the weakness of mankind's flesh where there is sincere commitment to seek after him in truth. God searches the heart and will give the struggling but sincere believer the necessary wisdom to overcome areas of weakness in his life. Overcoming sin does not happen in a vacuum. Every believer whether young or mature in faith, must be in the habit of praying for wisdom and spiritual strength so as not to submit to sin. Submission to sin makes the sacrifice of Christ to be of no avail and keeps man in a non-redeemable spiritual state. He that knows better but submits to sin will remain unfulfilled in life for he will not be able to receive what he could have had. Earnest and sincere prayer as it turns out is the key that opens the door that leads from the imperfect into the perfect.

Sin is that which the believer does which God has commanded him not to do. It can also be that which he refuses to do that God has commanded him to do. Sin takes man outside of God's will where he is vulnerable to predation by the forces of darkness. The faithful must always appropriate the blood of Christ through prayer so that he can have power and control over sin. He must appropriate the power in the blood so as to withstand evil. He must appropriate it so that he can find release from that which has hitherto bound him. He must appropriate it for he cannot win his spiritual battles any other way.

The faithful believer appropriates the power in the blood

of sacrifice by faithful obedience to Truth in the light of Christ. Christ Jesus occupies a very exalted place in the Divine fold from where he speaks on behalf of mankind. He is the best advocate that the sincerely repentant can ever hope for because he can relate as well as have compassion for mankind's weakness. Sin can be generalized in two categories. One category kills the spirit whereas the other wounds it. The sins that wound the spirit choke or make the power of God to be of minimal effect in the life of the transgressor. Sin that kills the spirit disconnects the sinner totally from God's will and redemptive power. There is no hope left for the spirit that is dead but that which is wounded can be rehabilitated.

Christ advocates for the wounded in spirit who is repentant. But he can do nothing for him whose spirit is dead on account of the rejection of the redeeming light of Truth through pride. To be cut off from God's will is an undesirable state to be in. Christ, who has insight into all things, for nothing is hidden from him, ceases to be an advocate where pride rules the heart. He that is filled with pride often ends up expending much energy with little to show for his efforts because God resists such as he is. Futility is often the result when man lives outside of God's will for the Holy Spirit will be offended and not aid him.

The sinner that has rejected Truth will be like one that is trapped in a ditch searching for a way to climb out. He is trapped in that state because he has thwarted God's plan by not following commandments. The seeker after Christ is commanded not to sin but yield to God's will as the sovereign guide of life. It is by obedience to God's commands that the faithful is spiritually affirmed and strengthened. It is by obedience that the spirit within is confirmed to be perceived by believers as belonging with the Divine. In effect, the faithful comes to know and be known in light when he is truly obedient to the will of God.

The caring and searching eye of God is always watching from above over his own below for that is the nature of his doting love for the beloved. Everything that mankind does on earth is recorded in Heaven either to his credit or discredit. In that wise, every true believer is called to live in holiness, sobriety and yield to God's will to be assured of a good record in Heaven as he completes his earthly round. He who yields to the guiding light of Christ will be molded into a vessel worthy of honor that will exceed expectations and be assured of a good record. His time on earth becomes purposeless for mankind if the record of his activities fails to meet Heaven's approval. It is by those records that all will be judged. As much as possible, the contents of each man's record must aggregate into a composite that mirrors the life and work of Christ Jesus while on earth. The profile of Christ is an unchanging template and should define the life of every true seeker.

God always makes a way available so that the faithful believer can escape temptations. He uses the power of the

Holy Ghost to bring into effect a sort of feedback mechanism by which the believer is kept from straying beyond the safe margin of his sovereign will. It is through the Holy Ghost that the errant believer is made to become aware of his transgressions. He that is convicted at heart and ceases from straying further before it is too late has been well served. The Holy Ghost serves the impulse of a caring and loving God who will not allow the repentant to perish but rather redeem him in love.

It takes love in the light of Christ to keep believers within safe margin and in communion with the Divine. Beyond the safe margin of divine oversight is a region where death abounds and the spirit of life does not exist. It is the place where angels fear to tread and must be avoided at all costs by those who love life. The flashes, convictions, promptings and information borne by the Holy Ghost cannot be received in that region for it is a dead zone. It is the gulf too wide to be bridged. Rejecting Truth offends the spirit of life and causes God's hand of protection to be withdrawn. When that happens, all hope is lost and that which is left is not salvageable but only good for the fire. The redemption story is that of lost souls found and brought back to the heavenly Father through love and Truth. It is only when his long lost ones are brought back home to the heavenly Father in love and Truth that the perfecting of mankind into divinity can run full course.

Chapter Highlights

- ✓ The believer that grows to full spiritual maturity becomes a vessel set aside for glorious service.
- ✓ He that grows to full spiritual maturity must use the power of God's anointing for divine glory.
- ✓ The world's hatred of the lover of Truth is good testimony about the presence of Christ within him.
- ✓ The believer whose mind is cleared of unwanted debris is freed from that which inhibits clear vision.
- ✓ The good in life belong in the treasure chest of the near and dear with due thanksgiving to God.
- ✓ God searches the heart to give true seekers wisdom to overcome areas of weakness in life.
- ✓ Sin takes mankind outside of the will of God where he is vulnerable to the prince of darkness.
- ✓ There is no hope for the spirit that is dead but that which is wounded can be rehabilitated.
- ✓ The unfaithful that disobey God's will expend much effort but have little to show for it.
- ✓ The faithful believer comes to know and be known when he is truly obedient to the will of God.
- ✓ The faithful is kept within a safe margin and from straying off course through the Holy Ghost.
- ✓ Man may be God's favorite creation but the Father will not shed his glory on the unfaithful.
- ✓ Man's perfecting in divinity can only run full course when God's lost ones are brought home to him.

From the deep and exhaustless

That's the treasure trove of love

The sweeter comes to abound

As bitterness vacates the heart

Chapter 11

AN ACCEPTABLE THRESHOLD

Perfecting in divine love is a continuous and custom fitting process. It is the measuring of the signet ring of Providence and the sizing of the robe of eternity. It is like the purification of gold. There is no absolute mark to define perfection in light but there is an acceptable threshold to be met. The journey continues for the seeker even after he has met that threshold to be joined in spirit and received by the Father. The perfecting process entails continuous observations made from Heaven above and relayed to the faithful believer on earth to prevent him from wandering outside of God's will. It is information availed by the Holy Ghost in timely flashes that only the tuned in spirit can receive. These promptings of the spirit afford insightful knowledge to help the believer avoid pitfalls and deal better with the issues of life.

The Holy Ghost originates from the vantage point of Heaven and aids the spiritually matured in Christ as he navigates through life on earth. 'He', being the Holy Ghost, helps to effect the perfecting of the believer while he is yet on his earthly journey. In countless ways, the Holy Ghost helps to prepare him for the task at hand, make corrections as necessary or change course if need be. 'He' enables believers to be privy to God's will so that they can be of the utmost service in the kingdom of light. 'He' enables the worthy to overcome challenges in areas of faith, family and earthly endeavors. In effect, the Holy Ghost helps to shine a brighter light as the harbinger of greater dawn to guide the faithful in glorious light.

The promptings and information received through the Holy Ghost by the faithful is like memos from God's heavenly throne to those tuned to receive. Such memos when received by the faithful must be acted on as the work of faith often misunderstood and much argued about. Heavenly memos serve to prompt the believer to activate and put his faith into action. Each memo received is a command that must be obeyed even though it may not seem like the right course of action to take. The imperceptible person may deride and decry such memos but they often turn out to be the way by which God uses the faithful to do the amazing to behold. It is by such that the impossible become possible for the obedient.

God's spirit always searches the heart of the faithful so as to remain informed about his desires. 'He' being the spirit determines what is needed but yet lacking for the believer in order to help him achieve his heart's desires. After a determination has been made, Providence then comes into effect to work things out so that the believer can achieve the desired outcome expediently. The outcome is always glorious when and where there is divine intercession to help mankind achieve his goals in life. Divine intervention serves not only to meet needs but to guide every step taken in the way after Christ so that the true seeker is never lost along the way.

Information availed by the Holy Ghost helps the receiver to change self and environment as well as leave a trail of enlightenment everywhere on earth. It is only with the aid of the Holy Ghost that mankind can model the heavenly way on earth to live from glory to glory thereby. Living from glory to glory is divinely appointed for the faithful through the Holy Ghost. The Holy Ghost not only brings comfort, joy and fulfillment but makes all things to be known in true light. It is by the Holy Ghost availed in love through Christ that helps make God real for the faithful.

Dreams, visions, flashes of inspiration during quiet times all add up to enrich the spiritual experiences in the way after Christ. The seeker must always live by Truth so that the enemy who often masquerades as a messenger of light can always be exposed to never put a blanket over his eyes. To abide in Truth is very important as it helps to sort out dreams, visions and mental flashes or intrusive thoughts where the enemy may attempt to sneak into the mind to mislead the believer. Whoever embraces Truth will be embraced by same. He will come to know as he is known for Truth is the mirror in which all things are revealed. He within whom the spirit of Truth has come to maturity will be guided by the Holy Ghost to see through every situation for what it truly is and be hardly deceived.

It is not possible to deceive the matured in Christ on account of the spirit of Truth that has come to full life within them. The faithful who lives by Truth has God's seal of approval as well as divine protection. The power of God shows forth mightily to make countless things possible where Truth governs life's endeavors. Truth leads from the night time to the dawn of the glorious morning but the faithful must brave the journey through the darkness of the world's hatred. The passage from darkness into light can be bewildering but it is the only way to retrace the footsteps of Christ and lead the seeker back to God.

The places and time may be different but the symbolism and figures remain the same. The passage from the world's darkness into heavenly light requires that certain men pass through certain places to encounter certain events. Certainty and safe passage from darkness into light only comes about by choosing God over the world. When the divine way is chosen, it leads ultimately to a new birth or regeneration if followed faithfully to the end. The life and teachings of Christ Jesus epitomize the divine way and provide the template for a successful navigation through the precipitous terrain that the world presents for him who seeks to ascend the mountain of faith. At the summit of the mountain is found Heaven's tableland that is the preserve of the starry in spirit. It is the abode of those who serve God faithfully so that their works shine before men. It is the place of true and pure light. The commandment for all who seek after the enlightenment of Christ is the same and timeless. The follower after the footsteps of Christ must love God. God is truth and therefore the seeker must embrace and live by Truth. It may be costly to love Truth in today's world but the gain of eternal life and connection to the Divine are priceless.

In addition to the love of Truth, the seeker must also love his fellow man for it is what defines Christ and brings mankind closer to God. The seeker must treat everyone as he himself would like to be treated for what affects one affects all in the grand divine scheme. The seeker who aspires for greater enlightenment must begin with the lesser enlightenment that is within his reach. He must prove faithful with what he has at hand before he can gain access to that which is not yet within his reach. He must start as a candle before he can become the lamp. He must be the lamp before he can become the 'sun'. He must be the light in a dark world and learn to make accommodation for the ignorance of the spiritually blind who do not yet know. He must learn not to turn his back on blind mankind but must walk towards those without wisdom so that they may learn from him. He must never be tired of washing the feet or correcting the wayward in the light of Truth and with love.

The faithful will often be misunderstood and misjudged during his time of labor. But events and time will vindicate him as well as validate his efforts for there is nothing carried out in true light that is wasted. The faithful must live to serve as God directs his heart. Neither the praise nor condemnation of men should motivate the man that seeks after God's approval and commendation. The faithful believer is enthroned by the Father through sharing in grace and must withhold nothing from anyone willing to receive in love. To do otherwise is to deny Christ and set grace to naught. The faithful must not try nor can he be able to turn off the fountain of grace but leave judgment in God's just hands. The believer is only an outlet and not the source of grace. He is only a vessel that holds the content and not the source. He has no choice in the matter until the things concerning Christ is brought to an end by divine mandate.

The hardship suffered by the seeker after Christ leads to the door of God's heart and pales in comparison with the rewards. The believer that seeks after Christ must always bear in mind that the way up is through the lowly. It is good reason for the brother of a low degree in Christ to rejoice in that he has been exalted in the heavenly way. The seeker is pruned of the wanted but unfulfilling so that only the needed and fulfilling will remain in his life. He must persevere for he will become a self-contained seed of the divine prepared to produce many good fruits in due season. He will pass through many foreboding valleys in order to make it to the exalted heights where the starry in spirit congregate. In the very dark moments when all will seem to be arrayed against him, the true seeker might think that he is the only one left who has made a full commitment to God. But that is far from the truth for the night sky has been filled with the stars of Heaven. The stars are the noble of soul who are committed to God and persevere through adversity to be reborn in light as sons of the Father. Such are the starry in spirit that abide under the shadow of the wings of the Almighty Father as the seminal seed for the beginning of the next age.

It is not easy for the sons of light to live in the world for they are indeed strangers passing through on their journey back to a heavenly home. The enemy of light knows who the sons are and will throw his worst at them. The sons are subject to much pestering and thorny issues in the flesh. But God does afford them sufficient grace to bear their cross to ultimate victory. It is all part of the purification and perfecting process that helps to transform mankind into the likeness of the Divine. The flesh has to become inconsequential so that the spirit within can fully abound. It is only when the flesh has been mortified that the spirit can become ascendant.

It is of great importance that the faithful in Christ seek a quiet and peaceable life. He must do all in his power to sow and nurture the seed of peace in good faith. The fullness of the riches of God can only be accessed by the spirit that is at peace. Only the spirit that is at peace can live above the world in an exalted spiritual state. To live in an exalted spiritual state is to dwell in Jerusalem and to have access to Zion. He that dwells in Jerusalem is in a beloved place where God will always grant his wishes.

Those who are dearly beloved by God often appear to be little before the worldly and are not often perceived as should. He that is dear before God is a son of mercy who is a giver in a world of takers. It is for the sons of mercy that God has saved the best for last. Only to such does he give good gifts for they have proven to be good custodians of that entrusted to them. The fulfilling and enduring gifts as well as judgment are entrusted to the merciful in spirit by the Father of all. Christ is a giver full of grace and ever willing to share. And so, all who are deemed worthy in his light are divinely appointed for a portion in mercy. Every laborer who labors not for man or self but for God is appointed for a portion in mercy for selfless service rendered in love through Christ. And so, God never withholds his gifts from the worthy in the light of Christ for they diligently attend to the heavenly business above all.

Chapter Highlights

- ✓ The perfecting process is a continuous and custom fitting process not unlike the purification of gold.
- ✓ God always makes provision so that those that serve him can be equipped to fulfill their calling.
- ✓ The faithful leave a trail of enlightenment on earth to define the heavenly way for others to follow.
- ✓ The faithful believer embraces and lives by Truth through Christ so as to be embraced in kind.
- ✓ Truth leads through the darkness of the world's rejection into the light of God's glorious dawn.
- ✓ The life and teaching of Christ provide the template for a successful navigation of the earthly passage.
- ✓ The believer who aspires for the greater must first do well with the less that is within his reach.
- ✓ The faithful that desires to be exalted must be pruned of such that drags down the spirit.
- ✓ God affords the faithful in Christ sufficient grace to bear his cross to ultimate victory.
- ✓ The faithful keep the trail of enlightenment open much like others before them kept it open.
- ✓ It is in the spiritual union of Father and sons that divine power shows forth mightily.

The simple life in orderly living

Affords fulfillment for mankind

Puts focus on the things above

With little care for things below

Chapter 12

THE KEEPER IS WELL-KEPT

All who are reborn in divine light have been remade in the image of God through Christ to serve the cause of Truth on earth. Such are bestowed with strong faith so that they are well fitted to serve God's divine will gloriously. The nature of their calling is to serve in love through Christ to the benefit of humanity at large. The reborn in spirit embody rain divinely availed that falls both on the good and the wicked. Such that are reborn in light were once sinners dead in spirit like many in the world today but came to recognize the error of their ways to change course in good order. They heeded the voice of Truth within to welcome Christ into the heart so that the old sinful nature in them has given way to be replaced by the new modeled after Christ. The new inner man is appointed to grow to full spiritual maturity in Christ in accordance with God's will. Not all who follow after Christ will attain spiritual maturity. Some will and others will not. But for those who do, Christ reappears within them to do God's bidding in the same anointing and power.

The anointing and power is the same and flows from God to the reborn in full light of Christ regardless of time, place or person. No man has seen God but the faithful in Christ experience him through the spirit as an unseen hand or impulse that guides mankind's earthly affairs. The faithful believer that is matured in Christ lives in an exalted state of spiritual awareness where his experiences with God are intimate and profound. Such are always divinely appointed or elected to hear and see in spirit for others. Many staked their lot with the world and care little about heavenly matters. Therefore they cannot perceive in true light but have rather become spiritually blind, deaf and dumb. It becomes incumbent on the spiritually matured in Christ to help guide those that are blind and still stumbling in the world's darkness into true light. The reborn have ascended to the mountain top and have overcome the world. They must go back down to the valley where the mission to rescue the blind and lost awaits. The reborn in light are given to live simple lives organized to seek God's face and to share the light of Christ. They may live in the world but they know that they are not of it. For all intents and purposes they are just passing through as citizens who have already received the passport to the heavenly home.

The sons of Heaven have been well prepared in spirit to help rescue those pre-destined for salvation but stranded and adrift in the world. It is urgent in the divine scheme that those earmarked for salvation by the Father be rescued to find redemption through the light of Christ. It is for this mission of providing guidance to those willing to embrace Truth in the light of Christ that the sons have been prepared. It is for that reason that they must maintain their spiritual worthiness and remain clean vessels ready for use by God. They must remain undefiled from the corrupting influence of the world. They must maintain their spiritual anointing in good care for such is a precious and rare gift. It takes divine anointing for the words that they speak to remain effective in accomplishing the desired end. Unless maintained in good care and good light in this wise, the redeeming power of the word of Truth will be dulled and be of no effect to help the lost. The call to help in the rescue of the lost is God's calling on the faithful. It is the burden of love for the young and blind placed on the shoulders of the elders in faith. It is such selfless sacrifice that brings pleasure to God to duly evoke the sweet smelling fragrance of eternity.

The glory of this world is surely and steadily passing away as each new day dawns. Hardly much is fulfilling, sustainable or enduring anymore as things keep falling apart. Things that were valued in yesteryears no longer hold much value today. The things valued today will definitely have little value tomorrow. And so the bane of wanting, hasting and wasting bedevils the world today because mankind refuses to put God first. God's gifts have great intrinsic and timeless value. Whereas the things of the world wane in value with the passage of time, divine gifts increase in value as the days unfold.

God is not just about the past and present but about the future on to eternity as well. Therefore heavenly gifts are true gold tried and purified in Truth. Such are everlasting gifts bestowed on the faithful as divine dew to nourish and enrich the life of the receiver. The faithful called to serve in true light must be guarded at all times for the prince of the darkness of this world remains determined to rob mankind of such gifts. It is on that account that the faithful must remain sober and be vigilant for the enemy is always probing for spiritual weaknesses to exploit. The reborn in divine light may seem little in the eyes of the world and be overlooked by many. Yet each son is the depository and divine vessel for realizing the riches and promises of God to mankind. That which God has promised in love is what the enemy is out to rob if he can or corrupt if he cannot.

The faithful that has been remade in the image of Christ must be very patient and long suffering for his task is often dismissed. Many may not thank or exalt him but God is always mindful to fulfill his desires. He must be resigned to share the Truth about God many times over as the case may be and love urges. In essence and its core, the message of Christ is very simple but it requires trust to embrace. Everyone is a sinner and spiritually dead. No one can redeem himself except God who indeed can save the sinful. It takes a blood sacrifice acceptable to God to absolve man of his sins. Because of God's loving nature, he has provided Christ as the lamb of sacrifice sufficient to foot the bill for the willing to enable him find justification. Where there is one justified by God, he will be perceived by those who love Truth and seek after true light. Wherever such are perceived, those that follow in his footsteps can find justification also if that is God's will.

The journey of spiritual transformation is fascinating but it is simply a tale of the seed planted in the faithful heart that grows into a tree of righteousness. The different stages of spiritual transformation can be gleaned from writings of the Apostle Paul as laid out from the book of the Galatian through to the Thessalonians. At the onset of spiritual transformation or stage of the Galatian, the new way of life beckons the seeker after Christ but the ways of his old life still has a strong hold on him. As he endures, the new begins to take hold even as the old ways keep trying to pull him back. It is the song of the sirens that sink many a mariner on the sea of life. He that escapes the siren songs of his old life can then grow to where the ways of the new take deeper roots and the old is uprooted. This is the stage where the beast of the old ways is subjugated and the spirit of God begins to govern the life of the seeker. Here is where the seeker begins to have concrete but limited spiritual experiences. There is great enthusiasm here as the seeker begins to realize that though he may be unseen with human eyes, God does really exist and his words are true.

The young believer is at very great risk at this point for the enemy wants nothing more than to forestall his enthusiasm for God and cripple his faith. It is at this stage or that of the Ephesian that the seeker after Christ learns to put on the full armor of God for that is his only chance of moving forward. He has to learn to eschew contention, be truthful, do right always, fully trust in God to do as promised, speak as the divine urges him and live for hope of eternity with the Creator as life's crowning glory. He that remains faithful and diligent in this wise will progress to the stage of the Philippian where he starts to attempt to win other converts to Christ for he can now testify about God based on his spiritual experiences. He will face discouragement here for he will realize that many will not share his enthusiasm for God. As a matter of fact, many including friends, family and acquaintances will reject the new person that he has become in Christ rather preferring the old man of the world that he used to be.

Sadly, this is a place of spiritual stagnation for many who profess to follow after Christ. Many often end their spiritual growth at this stage, foregoing full maturity to be stuck in grace. This is where many choose to repackage and sweeten the message of Christ for mass appeal. Jesus becomes a brand name to be exploited commercially. The message of salvation and the importance of affording a place in the kingdom of God becomes an enterprise to be exploited by man for financial gain. The quest for spiritual rebirth is soon exchanged for religious pomp, ceremonies, size of congregation and opulence of the place of worship among other things that matter little to God. The message changes from an emphasis on the spirit within to the material bounty availed through grace so that the frills of religion soon occupy primary focus with salvation of soul and eternity with God more of an afterthought.

When the message of Christ turns into an enterprise, it becomes more about the church of bricks and mortar instead of the living church that is without walls. The church without walls is the congregation of the spirits of just men perfected by following in true light after Christ Jesus. The living church is realized at the top of God's mountain after full spiritual transformation. The stage of the Philippian is not full transformation but two-thirds of the way up and a ledge where many seekers settle. Full spiritual transformation is that which should be desired.

Only those able to overcome the lust for fame and fortune can progress further. The lust for fame and fortune is the great trap that most professed believers are not able to overcome. Wherever lust after fame and fortune become paramount, the enemy of God is inadvertently enthroned. The stream of the restorative power of God will begin to recede to be soon replaced by upheavals and storms for God is being prostituted therein. He that truly loves wisdom must know that the lust for earthly possessions binds the soul and blinds man's spirit to the Divine.

A faithful few do trade fame and fortune for a place at the divine feast. These faithful ones are soon led into that certain peace which passes understanding. He that has found that peace is a spiritual dweller in Jerusalem for whom it is ordained to see many good days in life. The good days are moments in man's earthly sojourn when God intercedes to do the amazing and miraculous in his life. The faithful few who dwell spiritually in Jerusalem are the vehicles that God uses to accomplish works of glory on earth. They are the ones who can truly declare that they can do all things through Christ. They are the faithful few who duly progress from Philippians to become Colossians.

The Colossian is a spiritual giant who has met up with Christ and is a master of the mysteries. He has ascended to the summit of God's mountain to be justified before God and is privy to things veiled to other men. It is a climb of at least seventeen years for the seeker to mature fully as a colossus of faith. However, he that has ascended to the mountain top is called to descend to the valley to help show others the way up. He is called to walk towards those without wisdom and share that which has come to full life within. Indeed, the kingdom of God is found at the mountain top but the other things that will be added to it are found in the valley below. The Colossian is asked to become the messenger of God that traverses the heavenly and earthly to serve humanity in love. It is in the fulfillment of this service that the Colossian becomes the Thessalonian to live as a man under the mantle of divinity.

Chapter Highlights

- ✓ The sons of God have been prepared in spirit to live and act as Christ would as his spiritual clone.
- ✓ The sons live simple and organized lives configured to seek God's face and share true light among men.
- ✓ The burden laid on the elder in faith is to seek out and help rescue those lost in the world.
- ✓ The things entrusted by God to man have eternal value for such are tried and proven in Truth.
- ✓ God's gifts are everlasting and serve as divine dew that enriches and brings fulfillment to life on earth.
- ✓ Every son of God is a depository and vessel to help realize fullness of the riches and promises of God.
- ✓ The exalted before God must be patient and longsuffering for his duty is often unappreciated.
- ✓ The man justified before God is called to model the way of Christ for others to observe and follow.
- ✓ It is when the inner man begins to stir to life that dimness of soul is lifted from mankind.
- ✓ As the way of new life in Christ take deeper root, the old life has less attraction for the faithful.
- ✓ As the unfaithful seeks to pleasure the flesh, God increasingly becomes an afterthought in his life.
- ✓ The saintly serve humanity with unrequited love and are privy to conversations in heavenly places.
- ✓ God's kingdom is found at the top of the mountain but the things added are found in the valley below.

Fate and fortune of humanity lie with the young

But the prince of darkness lures them away easily

With such noise and twinkling lights that bewitch

Amid false promises that betide many with woes

Chapter 13

PLACE OF THE SELFLESS

The noise and the twinkling lights of the world present a formidable obstacle for the spiritually young to overcome. Nevertheless they have to be weaned away from its deceitful allures and the darkness that it portends into the light of Christ if mankind's future is to be salvaged. Patience and long suffering love is essential in order to breast feed the young with the word of Truth. There is much burping and throwing up in the way when dealing with the young in this wise but love never counts costs or complains nevertheless. The enemy is continuous seeking to corrupt the mind of the young who are often attracted to short cuts, likely to cut corners and bend the rules. Unbeknown to the young, there is no quick and easy way to realize the precious in life or attain the good and perfect. There is no quick way to meet up with Christ and no short cuts to be taken in the divine way. It is a long arduous climb to escape the world.

All who hope better for humanity must have a hand in molding the young through the forgiving light of Christ. It is by such that the Holy Spirit is availed to make spiritual transformation possible so the blind can begin to perceive in true light. It takes the Spirit of God to induce the young to open his heart to welcome Christ therein. It also takes same to avail spiritual strength to every laborer that labors in love to nourish the young in faith. The effort to reach the young through Christ will not only be discouraging but unfruitful as well without the intervention of the Holy Spirit. Only the latter can induce mankind to seek after spiritual rebirth through Christ but first a sower must plant the seed of hope in minds before that can take place.

The mission of Christ is that of life and love. It is to share the message of hope in good faith so that the Holy Spirit can do the work to turn the young believer on to new life. Without someone there to preach no one will come near enough to be reached. The young believer on his part must be diligent to nurture the good seed planted in him so it can attain full maturity in loving truth. Only by such can faith be put to work to produce good fruits and only by such can the young mature to find enlightenment. But the notion of seeking after an unseen God as life's priority seems illogical to the young. Such feel an urge to make a name in the world and so given a choice, opt for fame and fortune first over reconciliation with God.

Yet the Spirit of God never fails to win the earmarked but erstwhile lost, whether young or old, back to God's good grace as due as long as there is one matured in Christ that is acceptable. The challenge that faces the matured in Christ that has been to the mountain top is to correct the flawed teachings of those stuck in grace and indolent in the way of Christ. The mountain top is the place of greater enlightenment. The challenge that has to be met is how to bring the greater to where men have only known the lesser. This is the challenge that Onesimus faced when he had to return to the congregation of Philemon after being filled with greater enlightenment through the Apostle Paul. Onesimus had to return there in order to bring new life back to that which was once promising but has become moribund. The moribund will lack the healing balm of Christ and the spiritual wherewithal to aid the sojourner complete his earthly passage home to Heaven. Those left in the moribund will be stuck in an arrested spiritual development. It takes one who has been to the mountain top to revitalize the dying for only he has the greater vision and strong faith needed for regeneration.

The congregation of Philemon symbolizes all who are left in an arrested spiritual development. Such are filled with the old wine of lesser enlightenment. Onesimus is the believer who left the milk and sought after the meat of the word. He is the faithful and trusting believer who endured through adversity to be established from grace on to mercy. He is the faithful harbinger of greater light who has been prepared to bring illumination to that which is now mired in shadows. He who has been to the mountain top can clear the stream choked with the debris of misguided teachings. He can cause living water to start flowing again where it has dried up. He who has been to the mountain top has been to the abode of the clouds and is given to bring living water to the thirsty land.

The dry and thirsty place is often times the result of partial understanding and misguided love. Such is the case when mankind presumes to know more than he does or claims to be what he is not. Understanding in part rears the spiritual child into dwarfism and to unfulfilled hope. The spiritual dwarf will become blind to the true reality and possibilities of the kingdom of God. Consequently, he who should have become a man remains a child due to lack of better understanding. He settles in life as a man-child stuck in grace instead of a Christ-man that stands before God under mercy. The man-child of faith is unable to finish the race appointed for him in life for he has not known greater enlightenment and therefore is not able to make it to the mountain top.

The believer that has never been exposed to greater divine illumination will be limited in his knowledge of God. He will never have knowledge of the mysteries of the kingdom. He can only drink milk but cannot eat the meat of the word of God. The meat of the word is that which sustains to full spiritual maturity. The milk of the word does not and cannot do that. It takes one who has finished the race to afford the meat by which greater light is shone. He who has been to the mountain top will face much opposition from those who have never been. He is opposed because those who have never been to the top have not tasted the pure that flows directly from the heavenly throne of God. Those who have never been to the mountain top can never know in real time and in due season. Such who have never been cannot taste the new availed by the Holy Ghost in real time but can only regurgitate that handed down from the past.

Having not been to the mountaintop, the indolent in faith are clouds without rain that will not budge from their limited and misguided understanding. Having mastered the art of packaging the name of Christ for commercial appeal, they seek after the earthly rewards of fame and fortune. Such are the master salesmen of religion who build 'cathedrals of worship' as monuments to themselves in the name of Christ. But God is not looking for cathedrals to be built for him. Rather HE is looking for the faithful in Christ whose souls have been purified in the light of Truth. Such are the righteous in the way whose hearts have been washed and purified by Truth to become anointed vessels that HE uses to help restore lost souls through Christ.

The masters of religion have become princes in the world who rule churches of bricks and mortar as principalities. It is neither dark nor light in many earthly churches but a shadowy landscape. The laity hails these princes of religion as heroes as the sound of gold fills the air and tickles the ears. Unwarily and misguidedly, the people have entrusted their salvation to the hands of men instead of God. The Spirit of God becomes estranged wherever mankind has gone back to Babel in an impossible attempt to take earth to Heaven as found in today's churches of bricks and mortar. It is earth that has to be re-created in the order of Heaven and not the other way. It takes the Holy Spirit to translate Heaven to earth through the righteous that stand before God under mercy. Only the righteous before God can be used to model the heavenly way on earth. The insidious trap of marketing Christ for commercial appeal and material gain contrived by the enemy has proven to be very effective in blunting the true message of Christ.

The hunger for material reward does not reflect true living in the kingdom of God on earth. Rather spiritual transformation through Christ is. The kingdom of God is hidden from sight but spiritually perceived. It is the realm in which to achieve heavenly living on earth. God's will for mankind is for him to seek reconciliation with his Creator so he can receive sight as well as eternal life. Man must first seek the passport that warrants citizenship in God's kingdom before any other earthly pursuits. Every one that is fully matured in Christ has been elected by God to carry out a heavenly ordained purpose on earth. For every such elect there is an erstwhile lost or young believer earmarked for salvation that can only come to full maturity in Christ with the help of the one elected for him.

The fully matured in Christ must be diligent and persevere

in this divinely ordained purpose. He must carry on so that no one predestined and deserving in the way lacks the meat of the word of God needed for full spiritual maturity. Every elect has a harvest field set aside for him by God and will be held accountable for how well he performs in his calling. It is such labors carried out in the light and love of Christ that will define his finest moments on earth. Every elect one is chosen to serve those willing to trust in God's promise of love and goodwill for mankind. To serve in this light is the ordained mission which must come first before other pursuits in life. He who puts other pursuits aside to labor for God first will duly come into an existence where he is without lack in any area of life. Such is the lot of those that seek after the kingdom of God first for they will find same to have other things added to them in the end.

The kingdom of God asks of the fully matured in Christ to live to serve the young and the up-and-coming in faith. All who are fully matured in Christ are tuned in spirit to understand the language of life that ties all within creation together. Those tuned in this wise have received the gift of the Holy Ghost which the heavenly Father uses to make the needful known to all who are connected to him in spirit. It is for this reason that the fully matured in Christ are able to live in harmony with all in nature both as shepherds of the Father's flock as well as caretakers of garden earth.

Being shepherds of the flock of humanity, every elect one

is a householder who out of the treasure chest of his heart brings out things that are new but old. They are able to do so because God dwells in their hearts. Consequently they often speak about things that men's eyes have not yet seen or ears heard. In that light, the elect sons are God's gift to humanity as the seedling for the coming new age of Christ. They are keepers of the watch in the night time of humanity's missteps that sound the alarms that will save anyone who will listen. They speak about things that are at odds with mainstream thinking and current beliefs. They speak to the future and about unseen things knowable to only those who abide in the secret place of the Almighty.

God entrusts this sacred duty to those who are faithful to Truth. Such embody the mouthpiece to give voice on earth to the will of God who remains unseen but ever abides. Such are sealed in truth and immunized from the wickedness in the world. Often they speak about things that disquiet and discomfort the guilt ridden in the darkened chambers of the heart. There is no protection from its probing light when the elect speak Truth as God's faithfully urges them. The spirit of Truth does not speak to shame or deride but to remind mankind with unmistaken clarity that nothing is hidden from God's searching eyes. Truth only urges faithless mankind in love to change ways and seek God while there is still hope for redemption.

Chapter Highlights

- ✓ The enemy of light battles for the mind of the young for therein rests humanity's future and fate.
- ✓ It takes the Holy Spirit to make the young forego the worldly to seek reconciliation with God.
- ✓ The Holy Spirit never fails to lead the earmarked back to the path of reconciliation with God.
- ✓ The challenge that faces the faithful is to correct the flawed teachings of the indolent in faith.
- ✓ Those filled with the lesser enlightenment of the old will be in arrested spiritual development.
- ✓ Many who profess to walk after Christ are blind to the reality and possibilities of the kingdom of God.
- ✓ God cares little for grand cathedrals but much for hearts purified in truth and righteousness.
- ✓ The kingdom of God is the realm for the faithful to realize heavenly living on earth.
- ✓ Every elect has a harvest field prepared for him and is accountable for how well he fulfills his ministry.
- ✓ Truth that discomforts the guilty in the darkened chamber of the heart serves to free his spirit.
- ✓ God makes provision for adequate witnessing and proper guidance for all who truly seek after light.
- ✓ The faithful that are sealed in Truth are immunized from the wickedness in the world.
- ✓ God entrusts the sacred to the faithful sanctified in Truth through the light of Christ.

The man that learns and takes to heart

To keep company with others in Truth

Soon comes to walk in divine company

And be counted worthy of greater love

Chapter 14

AN UNMISTAKABLE VOICE

The Spirit of God operates in the life of the faithful believer to teach, guide and comfort him through the earthly sojourn. As the faithful believer feeds on Truth, a transformation begins to take place in his inner man. This is the first stirrings of the spirit and comes about by grace through faith in Christ as God's lamb of sacrifice divinely fitted to restore men's souls to new life. The spirit so stirred up within will grow from this infant beginning to full maturity in Christ if faithfully nurtured and God's will allows it. Spiritual maturation is a process that takes many years of obedience to the word of Truth to complete. Even so there is a perfecting process that continues and never ends in the life of the faithful even after he has come to spiritual maturity in Christ. The perfecting process brings the faithful believer into an intimate knowledge and deeper spiritual experiences within God's bowel of mercy.

Full spiritual maturity in Christ is a very significant event in the life of the believer. It signals that such a believer has undergone a spiritual transformation that has totally changed him within into the new entity of Christ. He has been bestowed with the mantle of Christ which will be reflected in his daily life. He has received the mantle which radiates light from within so that those who come to him can be induced to see and know as they have never seen or known before. It is a spiritual state that can be likened to lying on the breast of Jesus. It indicates two hearts that have been joined together to beat as one. It is a spiritual bonding that nothing can separate based on mutual love for God. The off-spring of such a bond will embody the divine contained in an earthly vessel.

He that has become one with Christ is a vehicle chosen by God to translate the heavenly way on earth. Only a chosen number will make it to full spiritual maturity to become one with Christ. The thoughts, words and actions of such will be exclusively governed and subject to the sovereign will of the Father. The heavenly Father is well aware of the limitations of man's flesh so that the perfecting process remains at work even for the fully matured in Christ. The heart that has become one with Christ will have same compassion and feelings in all matters as he does. The essence of Christ is compassion and accommodation for men's weaknesses. In so doing man honors the wishes of God that each man should be his brother's keeper. The heavenly Father has reserved an exalted place for the man that is his brother's keeper within the framework of creation. God keeps the man who is his brother's keeper.

By wallowing in the mud of sin and fleshly lusts, sinful man has debased himself and lost his place in creation. It takes the light of Christ and his loving compassion to change mankind from a debased state to a purified being worthy of keeping company with God. The faithful believer that learns and loves to keep good company with his brother in the light of Christ will come to keep company with God in due time. It is from this exalted place that Adam fell for God desired and looked forward to keep company with him daily. It is to this exalted place that the spirit of the faithful believer can be lifted up again when purified in the light of Truth and covered by the blood of Christ.

He that keeps company with the Divine has mounted up with wings of the eagle to the exalted realm. He that can mount up in that light can soar to the realm where those that have overcome the world congregate in spirit. The exalted realm is the spiritual habitation of immortal souls. The faithful mounted up thereon will have his heart beat with that of Christ and his mind connected with that of God. Such has been recreated in the image of Christ and divinely elected to carry out God's will on earth as love urges. Such is the lot of the faithful that has come into the congregation of the mighty. He must learn to stand to be counted worthy of that company. He must learn to stand even as the eaglet learns to fly. He must overcome his initial fears and venture beyond the known horizons. He must go beyond the gates for thereabouts is his portion. It has become appointed for him to step outside the box in order to excel in the glory of the heavenly son for he has broken the chains of mankind's mediocrity.

There is a post resurrection scenario in the last chapter of the gospel of John that is quite illuminating. Peter and a select company of disciples were on the shore of Lake Tiberias. They were engaged in a misguided effort to resurrect the life that they had before they became followers of Christ. Their encounter and time with Jesus had prepared them to be able to venture to a place beyond themselves but they had not yet realized that. They still looked to have their old lives back instead of reaching out for the new and better. They failed to realize that there is no going back when the seeker has bonded with Christ for then his hand is set on the plows of Israel.

Bonding with Christ requires much sacrifice in the way to be realized. For that reason, God no longer requires sacrifice of him that is so bonded but expects him to be merciful to the spiritually ignorant. There is no break to be taken when bonding with Christ takes place. It is a lifelong commitment that demands that the faithful love God with his heart, soul, mind and strength. He that is so bonded has joined the brotherhood where all men walk together in the spirit of fellowship with each other as sons of God. They have been called to join the band that plows together for God with the Christ Jesus as the leader.

The sons are banded together in spirit by love for the heavenly Father and a desire to please him. They neither seek the praise of men nor lust after such things as fame and fortune that motivate other men. Their desire and hunger to please the heavenly Father draws them ever closer to God where all hearts beat together in love.

The hearts that are close enough to God will always beat in harmony with the rhythm of Christ. The hearts that beat together evoke the spirit of universal brotherhood which is so elusive in the world today. But universal brotherhood is the motivation and main stay of the kingdom of God. The hearts that beat together function as transmitter-receivers that are broadcasting to each other and to others as well. They send and receive messages to and from others joined in this network of greater love wherein Christ governs all. The network of greater love is the realm of the kingdom of God where the faithful are tuned to a divine frequency kept aside by the heavenly Father for all whose hearts are ablaze with the flame of Christ. Though unseen, the connection and information shared therein is nevertheless real much like today's world of wireless communication where humans are immersed in a flood of data that only the suitably equipped can receive.

There is a perceptible light or aura of goodness that shines from within those who dwell in the kingdom of God. It is in this way that such are turned into beacons by which those that seek may come to know the way of love and peace. It is the righteousness of God imputed into those that dwell in his kingdom which evokes the light perceived. The faithful that are kept apart for use by God will have divine light shine forth from within their hearts and compassion to govern their actions. Their voices of compassion can never be mistaken for the truth of the message that they bear remains undeniable. The goodness and love for others by the messenger of Truth is always unmistakable. It is same Christ that shows up in all colors, tongues and cultures over endless ages. The believer who loves Truth can perceive him regardless of whatever guise or form that he appears in for Christ can always be known in spirit.

The profile of Christ is the same and so is his mission on earth among men. All who are bonded in Christ cannot help but have compassion for those spiritually blind to God's reality and power. Such live in sacrificial love and labor to bring others into true light and life. They cease not in their labor of love for they know that the welfare of all who follow in the footsteps of Christ is realized within a commonwealth of spirits bonded as one and governed by love for God. In this kingdom of light, all partakers are sustained by a common good availed through redeeming grace and divine mercy. In essence, the fellowship of Christ is a guild for receiving and sharing divine gifts with due thanksgiving to God so that goodness may abound forever.

Chapter Highlights

- ✓ The perfecting process avails intimate knowledge and deeper spiritual experiences about God.
- ✓ Full maturity signals spiritual transformation of the old within into a new entity in the light of Christ.
- ✓ The thoughts, words and actions of the faithful are governed by divine sovereign will.
- ✓ The sinful man debases himself and loses his place in creation by wallowing in sin and lustful desires.
- ✓ It has been appointed for the sons to break the chains of human mediocrity and excel in light.
- ✓ All who serve God must not look to have their old lives back but reach for the new and better ahead.
- ✓ God no longer requires sacrifice when man has given all so that others may come into true light.
- ✓ The sons are banded together in spirit by love and a desire to please the heavenly Father.
- ✓ The motivation and mainstay of the kingdom of God is truth and love by mankind for his fellows.
- ✓ There is a perceptible light of goodness that shines from hearts that dwell in the kingdom of God.
- ✓ Christ is a guild for receiving and sharing gifts with thanksgiving so that goodness may abound.
- ✓ The welfare of the followers after Christ is realized in a commonwealth governed by Truth and love.

The illumination received in a lightning streak

Much like inspiration that visits man in a flash

Is a potent sign in the Heavens to tell seekers

That all things are known in the light of Truth

Chapter 15

RICHES OF THE FIELD

James and John, the sons of Zebedee, are always referenced together in the scriptures for good reason. The name James speaks to that which is new, timely and fulfilling. It speaks to the refreshing and sustainable that will not wax old. The name John defines the gift divinely availed that is for the common good of humanity. When understood in this wise for what they stand for, then the symbiosis between the two names becomes clear. James defines the desirable and needed outcome which will never be invalidated. John, on the other hand, defines the divine impetus which makes that desirable and needed outcome possible. Every vessel kept apart for use by God is always sandwiched between the essence of James and John. John is the receiver or inlet for divine gifts from above and James is the dispenser or outlet. Put simply, the vessels of glory receive in mercy with the right from God and give to men in grace with the left in a rain cycle.

James and John are deservedly known as the sons of thunder. Thunder is that burst of energy which petrifies the fearful and ignorant. However the same thunder sparks lightning which flashes to offer enlightenment in darkness. Enlightenment brings clarity when minds are surrounded by the darkness of uncertainty. By and large, thunder also brings rain in its wake and aftermath to shower the patched earth. Same lightning that offers enlightenment also sparks fire that burns away the cluttered ground so that new life can have needed room to emerge. It has been mankind's age old quest and enduring wish to catch thunder in a bottle. He that is able to do so will no longer be in darkness but will have the vision to overcome obstacles and produce the new.

Thunder is that burst of energy which transforms the landscape when properly harnessed and channeled. Lightning and rain are the sons of thunder. As mentioned earlier, lightning offers glimpses of enlightenment during times of darkness. It heralds the spirit of life for it prepares the ground to receive rain. And so Truth prepares the mind to receive the living water that brings new life. Rainfall is the recyclable gift that brings life to make goodness abound. Rainfall makes it possible to be fruitful and multiply. Rainfall symbolizes grace and mercy which should be shared by all. Mercy can be distinguished from grace in that it is the latter rain which comes at the end when the need is dire and there is no other recourse. It is God's best saved for last for those who serve faithfully. All who are bonded with Christ are sandwiched between James and John. Such are given to hear the still small voice of God in spirit. He that is so tuned to the Divine must act in obedience to that which he has heard. He that hears the inaudible has received the Holy Ghost to inform and will be availed the Holy Spirit to enable him do the marvelous.

The name Simon defines one who hears God and Peter one who acts on what he has heard. The name Simon Peter therefore defines the representative model of the believer bonded with Christ who is sandwiched between James and John. It is for this reason that Christ Jesus called only Peter, James and John on certain occasions. 'Simon Peter' typifies the faithful believer who in his journey of faith passes through many peaks and valleys to finally come to rest in Christ Jesus. Through that process he becomes fully transformed in spirit as a son of light and a representation of the building block of the living church.

Only the fully matured in Christ can capture the lightning of veiled Truth in a bottle and not be torn apart. They that can receive such are special vessels prepared for the works of glory by the heavenly Father. They are vessels of honor set aside and meet for the Master to use in accomplishing his purposes on earth. Each such vessel is appointed to endure much tribulation on account of devotion to Christ and love for God. However it is by such tribulation that they come to afford the patience, spiritual fortitude, peace, and hope that make all things possible in Christ.

The special vessels are filled with the essence of Christ and divinely fitted with two handles. The right handle is the handle by which God touches the faithful to bless him and the left handle is that by which the faithful gives to the world. The faithful that is touched by God's divine hand is filled with the Spirit of the Father. John represents the right handle by which the faithful is connected to and receives from God. James represents the left handle by which the faithful carries out God's divine will on earth.

As mentioned earlier, the vessel well-fitted on both hands is well prepared to serve God's divine purposes among men as the building block of the kingdom of Christ. Every vessel well-fitted in this wise lives in obedience to that which God speaks into his heart through Christ. He lives to please God regardless of cost and injury for he figures that the heavenly Father knows best. Such has been recreated in the likeness of Christ and cannot help but obey the will of God. The preset roles of James on the left and John on the right hand are ordained to attend every vessel whose ways are pleasing to God. It is by this special dispensation that each vessel can evoke the spirit of thunder when they clap their hands in approval. It is a timeless role that has been set from the foundation of time. No one hand can evoke thunder or serve the divine purposes well on earth in exclusion of the other. It takes both hands clapping in God's praise to evoke the thunder that tears the veil of mystery to reveal the divine sovereign will to man. The scriptures implore one brother not to hate the other. It implores one hand not to oppose the other. It is the test that Cain the offspring of the first Adam failed. It is the same test that all offspring of the last Adam (Christ Jesus) must pass. Rather both hands must work together so that the love for God will prevail and the divine order may reign supreme for such is of the kingdom of God.

To live in the kingdom of God on earth is to live in the days of the second Sabbath and in greater enlightenment. The days of the first Sabbath are for men to learn the laws and ways of God. It is man taking the beginning steps towards reconciliation with God. The first Sabbath may be likened to the period when a child is learning the language of his parents. Once he has learned the language, he can then begin to put it to great use for he is now in possession of the key to decode his environment. A child who has been well taught by his parents has been empowered to process and understand his environment. He is able to 'hear' what everything in his 'world' communicates and is about. He can master his environment and will no longer need his parents to be able there to navigate his way within that environment. The days of the first Sabbath give man the chance not only to learn the words and way of God but to learn obedience. The diligent child who learns to live in obedience to the words of Truth taught him will come into spiritual maturity and be fruitful in every area of life.

Spiritual maturity affords the faithful believer the key to enter and flourish within the kingdom of God. Access into the kingdom of light avails the passport to eternal life. The benevolent hand of Providence will uphold all who have such access in goodness and mercy. He that has the passport of life will be used by God to change things for the better in many areas of life for those willing to receive Christ. Spiritual maturity evokes the thunder that rends the veil that separates the Heavenly and earthly. It is the earthquake that changes the human landscape for better. The faithful who is fully matured in Christ to enter into God's kingdom has come into a world of harmony and orderliness where divine purpose is the order of the day. Everything speaks, listens and works to fulfill God's order in this kingdom of light. In that realm, the common good is the motivation and love is the outcome.

The kingdom of God is the realm of the second Sabbath and the greater enlightenment where nothing ever dies. The days of the second Sabbath is the season in which the spiritually matured in Christ can partake with the other immortal souls to recreate in light. The faithful has to pass through the cross to be welcomed therein for there is no other way. His old self has to die through the crucible of the world's rejection but out of that ordeal he will emerge in new life to be afforded a place in the kingdom of light. The latter is where life has vanquished death for therein all things can be called forth to glorious life.

God's kingdom of light is the field of dreams where immortal souls congregate. It is the cornfield that can only be dreamed about by mere mortals but in which the fully matured in Christ come to find recreation in the company of immortals souls as sons of light. The recreation of the immortals is to bring new things out of the old. It is their pride and joy to make sure that nothing worthy of salvage is wasted in creation for such have been borne out of God's goodness to mankind. This field of dreams is the cornfield of amazement that is obscured to all but the pure of heart. It is the place of greater enlightenment revealed only to those that trust and obey God's commandments even as the dutiful child trusts and obeys the loving parent. It is the place of regeneration where the old come to be made new again. It is a place where nothing waxes old. It is much like a treasure chest out of which are brought out things that are new but yet old.

To whom much is given is much required. The corn field is an amazing place but it is for only the faithful who live for the goodness of humanity. He that lives to serve God faithfully does so in the hope of spending eternity with the heavenly Father after his service on earth is done. The corn field is the place to realize the good and perfect divinely availed as a foretaste of the Heavenly. It is the realm where the lowly in the eyes of men are exalted before God. It is the realm where the faithful are entrusted with the secret things of creation. This dream works of the greater enlightenment is reality for those reborn in the divine light of Christ. But it remains the place of dreams and the exclusive playing fields of 'gods' for those that are still mired in spiritual blindness.

The faithful for whom the field of dreams is real has ascended the heavenly highway to walk in the company of immortal spirits. He is a co-inheritor with the other sons of light of the fullness of the riches of God. Such has become adopted into the divine family as the justified before God perfected through Christ. All given to faithfully follow after the first born son Christ Jesus will become sons of the Father in this wise. It is a right of inheritance under divine mercy. Every son borne of light is connected to a source of infinite possibilities which never stops giving. He that is so connected can soar to the exalted heights to join in heavenly conversations as well as walk on earth as a man to accomplish God's divine purposes.

All reborn in the light of Christ as his sons have kept faith with God to be rewarded them with the language that he took away at Babel long ago and far back. He has given back each son the means to reach Heaven from earth. He has given them the language borne in the light of Truth with which to commune with him and with each other. It is language reserved for those who have scaled the summit of faith to be reborn as 'Christ'. Everyone that has scaled the summit is a golden spirit that can bring the priceless out of the common, the extra-ordinary out of the ordinary and the heavenly out of the mundane under divine mercy.

Chapter Highlights

- ✓ The sons receive gifts with due thankfulness from God and pass same on to others in comradeship.
- ✓ The enlightenment of Christ affords wisdom to those surrounded by the darkness of ignorance.
- ✓ Lightning is the emblem for spiritual enlightenment whereas rainfall portends fruitfulness.
- ✓ The faithful hear the still small voice of God and act in obedience as the building blocks of his kingdom.
- ✓ The faithful that is filled with the Spirit of God has captured that elusive lightning in a bottle.
- ✓ The heavenly Father anoints the worthy in Christ with the fragrance of sacrifice well-received.
- ✓ Every true son acts in obedience to what has been spoken into his spirit regardless of cost and hurt.
- ✓ Spiritual maturity evokes thunder that rends the veil which separates mankind and the Divine.
- ✓ The desire for common good is the motivation and love is the offspring in the kingdom of God.
- ✓ The field of dreams is obscured to many but revealed to those that are pure of heart.
- ✓ The faithful for whom the field of dreams is reality has gone beyond the horizon to become eternal.
- ✓ The righteous before God bring the priceless out of the ordinary and exalted out of the mundane.

To love the Truth and obey in light

Connects to the source of wisdom

And 'to creation's governing order

So that heart's desires can be had

Chapter 16

THE SWEET SPOT

There is a certain and definite order that governs all things in creation. That order was first set in place by God when he created the heavens, earth and everything contained therein. At the present time, it may all appear chaotic and confusing to the uninformed and spiritually blind but that is far from the case. God did not set about to create confusion and chaos as a final outcome. He is never taken by surprise either for he knows all the way from the beginning through to the end of all things. It should then be clearly understood that regardless of how things seem now, the underlying order set down from the beginning by God will prevail at the end when it matters the most. It will become evident to all then that God has always known what he is doing and remains fully in control even though it might not have been obvious to the faithless.

At the fulfillment of the time appointed for this age, all things that are left in creation will come into knowledge of their true place in the divine order. All who have passed judgment in God's eyes will be found standing when that time comes. They will be the ones deemed worthy of spiritual communion and eternal fellowship with the heavenly father. Such are the faithful in the way after Christ worthy to be transformed into his spiritual likeness. Such will continue in glorious fellowship with God as well as others that are righteous before him.

The righteous before him are chosen to be adopted into the divine family by the heavenly Father. They are chosen on account of a life of faithful obedience to the words of Truth and devotion in the way of Christ. Such are fused with the divine ethos because they have yielded to God's will as life's sovereign guide. They persevere to serve the divine will so that everyone that they encounter on earth may be nudged a little towards the Creator. In many ways, their lives on earth have been much like puffs of winds that uplift the willing towards the heavenly Father. Not everyone is receptive to Truth and willing to accept God's offer of redemption through Christ. The faithless that rejects Truth and the light of Christ is precluded from knowledge of the Father and joining the divine household. There is no other recourse for the precluded than for his moribund spirit to return to the base material of the earth. On the other hand the believer that is adopted into the divine family has become bound with God eternally. Such is man's lot when he has found salvation and settled into the place destined for him from the foundation of time.

The heavenly Father always does as he says and will never

do anything without letting his faithful servants know. One of the marvelous things about God is that he hates surprises and will always give advance warnings of his intentions. He will always signal his intentions to those who trust him for guidance. He hates to see anything and anyone in creation suffer needlessly if it can be helped. Sadly it is man that has left the place divinely appointed for him and gone his own way. Yet it is God's desire that those who have gone astray come to be duly reconciled with him. But he also knows that most love the world too much to make the commitment to seek that reconciliation.

But in his forgiving and loving nature, God is willing to suffer indignity in the hope that no true seeker after light is left without hope or stranded in the way. The spirit of the world is noisome so that confusion often reigns and drowns out his voice that pleads with humanity to change course. As one comes to believe in the teachings of Christ Jesus to let the words of Truth guide him in life, the noise of the world will begin to fade for him. He will come to be spiritually untangled from the clutches of the world and to enter into peace availed through Christ. It is in this state of peace that the seeker after Christ begins to be tuned in spirit to the Divine and to see God's handiwork in creation.

The believer begins to hear and see the handiworks of God clearly when he has become alive in the spirit of new life through Christ. It is in this place of spiritual communion that the true servants of God dwell. Since God will never do anything without letting the faithful know, he uses those tuned to him in spirit as his mouthpiece to speak to those that are not. He communicates his intentions to those who can understand him more clearly and uses them to speak to those who understand little about him or not at all. These oracles of God speak from a place veiled to most men but made known to only a few. They speak about things concealed to the earthbound in spirit. The message is often about the sad trend of things on earth and the impending doom for mankind due to his ungodly ways. Yet it always reminds about the gift of Christ as the way of escape from that doom into safe refuge with God.

It only requires the love of truth and belief in the teachings of Christ Jesus for mankind to find that escape and refuge with the heavenly Father. The faithful believer who is committed enough to embrace Truth wholly will be led in spirit through the straight and narrow that is the way of Christ. It is a 'worm hole' that leads away from a world of darkness into a world of light. It is the worm-hole that Jacob the earth-man of dust crawled through to come out transformed as Israel the god-man of glory. It leads from the world of mere mortals into the place of god-men beyond. It is made available to the faithful that seek after God in humility and sincerity for no one can find the way by the works of his own hands. Only those who love the way of Christ unconditionally are chosen and led to find it. The passage through the worm-hole is a gift received by faith through grace with God as the final arbiter.

The place of the god-men beyond where the true servants of God dwell can be likened to the spiritual house top of the earth. It is the top of God's mountain and heaven's table land. The faithful that dwell thereabouts can be likened to communication satellites positioned in that sweet spot between the earth and greater beyond. It is a place inhabited by the spirit that is truly at ease. It is reserved for the noble in spirit who put their trust in God. In putting their trust in God, the faithful do find that place of harmony where there is no perturbing the universal order within creation. They find their places in that order to become vehicles by which divine riches may be availed to mankind. They that dwell on the spiritual rooftops serve to give voice to those things heard with the ear of the spirit in divine light. They never speak unless it is for the common good and benefit of mankind. They will not proselytize their faith nor exploit it for gain. Such are the worthy trustees of divine gifts and faithful custodians of the precious with which they are entrusted.

He that dwells on the spiritual housetop occupies a very special place. His conversation will no longer be about the lowly that pervades today's world but about the heavenly purposed to uplift humanity. He that has joined the conversation in heavenly places is able to prophesy and speak about impending events before they come to pass. In today's world as the time of the fulfillment of all things approaches, he is able to speak about imminent things that are at mankind's doorsteps. He that will be effectively used in this way must get rid of the corruptible from his life. He must not come down from the 'housetop' to get that which he has left behind in the house. He must remain on the housetop so that he can be steeped in heavenly mists and divine dew. He must remain there so that he can be duly informed as well as have insight into the mystifying in life. In order to do so, he must let go of all that are earthbound so that he can stand in the congregation of the mighty for that is his destiny.

He who has grown to dwell on the spiritual housetop must live by the statutes of God. There are things intimately revealed that the faithful must safeguard and hold dear to heart. It is by those things that he will be known and judged. This is the 'Achilles heel' that he must protect so that he is not precluded from standing in the congregation of the mighty. He must observe the statute revealed to him for it is by obedience to such that the spiritual child becomes a man of God. The faithful in light who observes the statute appointed to him will become a statue fashioned in God's own true likeness. He will stand among the congregation of the valiant framed in peace and serenity for all ages to come. He will stand among the Colossus of faith for all who seek knowledge and wisdom to learn from. He will stand with his eye fixed above and will be counted among those who will catch the first rays of the break of mankind's glorious dawn.

The faithful who dwells on the spiritual housetop has

grown to maturity in Christ Jesus. He has chosen to forego all that will keep him earthbound so that he may escape to the exalted place appointed for him among the stars. For such, God's truth is life's guide for therein is woven the golden threads of the eternal that are for the exalted in spirit to truly and fully fathom. The exalted in spirit are able to fully fathom Truth because the wisdom therein is framed in pictures for them to perceive. This exalted place of spiritual escape is the meeting place between the Divine which reaches down from Heaven above and the hopeful spirit which reaches upwards from earth below.

The confluence of the heavenly and earthly is the realm of greater divine illumination. It is in this realm that the harmony of the scriptures can be fully understood and the infallibility of God's truth clearly ascertained. This is the realm where Hope speaks in the still small voice that can be heard and clearly understood within the spirit. It is in this realm that the Truth declared within the words of scripture and the experiences of daily life perfectly agree to confirm the reality of the Divine. The exalted realm is where the glorious concealed by God are known by the noble in spirit deemed of honor before him.

The statutes address the mundane that hold back the upward bound from ascending into the place of glory. The glory belongs to the heavenly Father but he is eager to shed it on those worthy in Christ. There is an appointed season when the seeker must forego certain things in order to come into the knowledge of the Father. It is then that the seeker through Christ separates himself from the world out of own volition so that he can intermeddle with all wisdom. Only in this way can the believer come to the fullness of the knowledge and wisdom of God. It is in this way that he will come into knowledge of God's will and the wisdom of all ages. It is the statute revealed to the faithful in Christ that separates him from all others and makes him to be of effectual use by God. It is the statute that makes him a certain man unto God. It is the statute that certifies that he has placed God above all things in his life. It is by the statute that the faithful is chiseled into a statue that fits into that certain cleft made in the Rock of Ages.

As noted earlier, there is a season of spiritual transition in which the spiritual child becomes a man of God. In that season, all that has been reserved for the faithful in Christ will become his to possess. The vessel must be clean in that season so that there is no corruption and defiling of that which he will be endowed with. There must be no unequal yoking or conforming to those around him who are unworthy of honor before God. This is the season for him to be transformed and he is called to leave those things that are not able to come up to housetop in the house below. He must therefore present himself as a living sacrifice dedicated to be used marvelously to Heaven's glory. He must be willing to step away from the present things that encumber his spirit so that he can be used to secure the future. This is his reasonable service for he has become a son of Heaven by whom many will experience spiritual rebirth and escape imminent judgment. He has also become a depository of the needful that those who have lived in pursuits of the wanted now lack and need. It is in this light and for this purpose that the dweller on the housetop has been chosen to serve as 'savior' for many.

The fulfillment of the events prophesied in earlier times and in the sacred books rest on the sons of Heaven. They are the vehicles or instruments used to make those things come about. They are players in the cosmic drama with significant roles to fulfill. They exercise their power and fulfill their roles through obedience to God's divine will. They constitute the spiritual bulwark that stand against the evil that constantly threatens mankind for their prayers and call to God for help do work wonders. For this reason they are given knowledge of certain events as well as called to share such in the hope that humanity can be spared from trouble ahead or blessed as the case may be.

The faithful entrusted with due knowledge by God labor under a heavy burden. It is a monumental responsibility for them to bear for oftentimes their warnings and counsels are often ignored. Such warnings are met with doubt, ridicule and derision from a dismissive world. The blind that live in a world of darkness can never experience the wonders of enlightenment unless they can be made to 'see'. And so the transformed in Christ, who is a creature of hope, never gives up trying to help the blind see while there is time left and work to be done. He responds to love's urge and spares no effort while there is still one left on the way to be rescued. Only when there is none left to be rescued will his work be done so that he can enter into the rest ordained for him by the heavenly Father.

The knowledge of events glimpsed from behind the veil by the faithful that dwells on the spiritual housetop must be written down faithfully so that there are never forgotten. Such knowledge is like the sprinkling of golden dust from Heaven. It must be safeguarded and put to the benefit of mankind as called for. In such knowledge is gleaned the substance of the everlasting and unchanging with which Heaven is populated. Such knowledge evokes and sustains life itself as well as power that makes old things new. The knowledge and wisdom of God revealed to mankind is solely for the purpose of redemption and rebirth. It assures victory in the battle of light against darkness where the soul of the next generation is at stake. The faithful who seeks after God in the light of Christ may suffer temporary loss in the world but in his house will be laid up much wealth. The wealth laid up therein is not the kind that the world affords but the true wealth that the noble in spirit seek after. These are the needful and enduring things that the predatory spirit cannot touch. These are the good gifts that the heavenly Father assures in love, ensures in light and insures by faith.

Chapter Highlights

- ✓ The underlying order set down from time by God will prevail once again at the end of this age.
- ✓ The faithful walk on earth so that the spirit of every man that they encounter is lifted towards God.
- ✓ The twinkling lights and noise of the world drowns out the voice that pleads with man to change ways.
- ✓ God communicates his intentions to the faithful to uses them to speak to the faithless and blind.
- ✓ The walk after Christ may be considered lowly by the world but it leads from darkness into new life.
- ✓ The sweet spot between the heavenly and earthly is where the order of creation is unperturbed.
- ✓ The faithful that dwells on the spiritual housetop will be steeped in knowledge and wisdom.
- ✓ There is a season to forego certain things in order to meet up with Christ and come into the Father.
- ✓ Duty calls the reborn in light to help others realize spiritual rebirth and escape divine judgment.
- ✓ The sons of God constitute the bulwark that holds evil at bay by their earnest entreaties and prayers.
- ✓ It is only when the faithful finishes the work ordained for him that he enters into faith rest.
- ✓ Wealth appointed for the faithful in light is assured in love, ensured in light and insured in faith.
- ✓ The battle of light against darkness is really for the collective soul of the future generation.

Many often seek and find fool's gold to heart's fill

Blind men who cannot see that the earth is a dump

Constantly being recycled by a non-wasting Minder

Who searches in light of Truth for the redeemable

Chapter 17

PEACE THAT IS PRICELESS

The enemy of Truth, who is the prince of the darkness of the world, is a liar and destroyer. His sole purpose is to lead mankind into a state of spiritual bankruptcy where the creature is honored rather than the Creator. When the creature is honored above his Creator, then the course of goodness is forestalled and the curse of evil installed. The enemy aims to achieve this evil plot by the spiritual strangulation of humanity's collective soul through crave for self-glory. He who loves to hear others sing his praise is a 'Herod' in spirit. Such will slaughter the next generation including his own children for short term gain. But the just that honor the Creator with due praise is given rather to save lives to Heaven's delight and glory. Love for self leads mankind to sacrifice the future for the present. But selfless sacrifices made for others assure welfare of the future.

The parent that is led astray by the enemy to love and hunger after the material above all things puts his offspring at great risk of spiritual death. In his distraction, the parent often fails to shield the child from the pervasive darkness and encroaching evil that often overtake the young. The enemy of light seeks to corrupt the fruit of the tree. He seeks to corrupt the children so that the collective soul of humanity's future is bound with him in the earthen bowel. The earthen is miry clay that besmirches the soul to entrap all therein in consuming convulsions of envy and strife. It is a place that knows no peace for therein all thrive on blame and writhe in pain. Life therein is a helter-skelter existence that can neither sustain nor produce that which is stable or enduring. It is a joyless place of the unpleasant, regrettable, bitter and woeful endings.

The way of Christ is a better choice for it is upward bound and yields the good fruits of peace as well as life. Many are blind to Truth and have rejected the upward way that offers escape from the earthen. Such have rather chosen to follow the downward thrust that keeps mankind earthbound. As a result of that choice, many have sacrificed the future of the children to a gloomy doom for the temporary gains and wanted things of today's passing world. With a traumatic end in wait, this world is not meant to be mankind's final destination. It is but a transit point from where those deemed worthy will be lifted up for the journey to man's true home in the starry heights. Only those who have sincerely sought after and found Christ are deemed worthy for a passport and ride home.

Man will always be a worm crawling in the miry dust of

the earth until he finds Christ the gateway to Heaven. As long as he is determined to search by his wits and on own terms, man will be like Jacob and never find the gateway. The conversation in heavenly places that he desires is not of the mind and flesh but in the spirit. Mankind can only find the gateway that leads on to the starry when he realizes that it is futile and to his spiritual detriment to wrestle with God. The worm hole or the gateway to the heavenly that leads to the starry realm is Christ. Mankind has to search in Truth with love for God in order to have a chance of meeting up with Christ. Not all who catch a glimpse of Christ will meet up with him to board the flight home for many are called but a few are chosen. Those left out will be unwilling to let go of the world in order to meet up to Christ. However some will be willing to forego all to meet up with Christ to board for home. The seeker who has found Christ will forever pass in and out through him to find fresh pasture in pristine fields. This will always hold true as each age ends and another begins. He that is framed in spirit by the door posts of Christ has come into regeneration and will always bring new things out of old.

He that has met up with Christ has become part of true Israel and the living church. He has become a prince of God among men christened in light as a savior to model the way to eternal life for many others. The truth about Christ Jesus has already been told and published for all to know. Mankind has been adequately and sufficiently informed about the gift of grace through Christ. There are many alive today who have found and passed through the door of Christ to take spiritual flight into God's kingdom of light. Those are the truly faithful who have spiritually matured through grace to live under mercy in the kingdom of light. Sadly most men are yet to afford this divine portion and have no knowledge of the place beyond. They consider themselves as having made it on earth and sit pretty well. Such are the damned and already condemned who have sought after and found fool's gold to heart's fill. They have failed to realize that the earth is a dump that will always be recycled. They have failed to realize that true gold is only found in the place beyond.

The truth is that the earth is constantly being recycled by the non-wasting heavenly Father who searches everything so that nothing redeemable and salvageable is ever lost. Sooner or later a point of no return is reached when all the recyclables have been redeemed and the collectibles salvaged with nothing left but garbage. At that point of zero return with nothing of value left, the garbage is burnt so that a pristine landscape can emerge. The regeneration of the earth in the order of Heaven begins with the 'collectibles' who have passed through the door of Christ as the founding seedlings. The garbage that will be burnt is that which did not pass judgment and is of no use in the new age where Christ will reign.

The dutiful and faithful few who have chosen the upward way of Truth have chosen wisely. They have not only received and treasured the teachings of Christ at heart but have shared it as the bread of life to nourish others in anywhere they can. Through their diligent service in love, others have come to embrace the way of Christ to be led to find peace and new life within the Divine fold. Those that prove to be faithful in the light after Christ will always have a place reserved for them around the heavenly table to dine in divine light. Such will always dine in wisdom with Christ Jesus for they have come into the everlasting where the enduring and fulfilling is found. They have escaped the spiritual trap of the earthen to find shelter in the heavenly and starry. Those that are sheltered therein have come into faith rest to have a glow that shines forth out of their starry spirits. It is light borne of the anointing of God to crown every soul deemed worthy of Heaven by God. The light from within or sun evoked in righteousness serves as a beacon to show the blind true way before hope is lost.

The 'sun' of righteousness duly arises within the hearts who have found the door of life to find escape to the heavenly. The 'sun' of righteousness has arisen in the hearts of the faithful who have taken spiritual flight up to the source of all light. Such are the justified before God unto whom it has been appointed to save the unwary from the slaughter being visited on them by evil shepherds. There is an unmistakable illumination wherever true light has risen that helps the spiritually blind to see in better light. They that bear true light span the bridge between the old and the new that the uncertain soul must cross so that his heart can settle on God. Such are the faithful by whom the children are shielded from drowning in the pool of spiritual malaise that surrounds mankind everywhere.

Every bearer of true light is to show the young the way so that their minds may be sharpened and their ebbing strength renewed. The righteous before God is called to be a spiritual Father unto many so that the bond of faith between the 'fathers and sons' may once again be established. This is the bond that assures the showers of blessing on humanity from the heavenly without which the earth remains cursed. The curse of the earth is seeded in that which comes from below for it is weighty and stops the spirit of man from reaching for the heavenly. But that which is received from above uplifts man's soul to afford him gifts that satisfy his longings for fulfillment and peace.

He in whom the 'sun' of righteousness has risen is a very exalted spiritual being. He is specially anointed in the spirit of God to bring light into dark and hidden places so that many can escape from the darkness to find new life in Christ. True light sends the enemy to flight from wherever he has found a home. It shames the enemy and renders him powerless when he is withstood by the true light of Christ. Greater love is that which fuels true light so that the nature of all things can be truly known.

He that looks into the light borne of greater love in truth will receive insight into himself. He will see what he is doing wrong and where he is going astray. He will come to know what ails him and find healing thereby. The bearer of true light goes where the Father sends in love. He is led in the spirit of God to offer up prayers and receive answers for the children in the way. The child is one, whether he is young or old, who comes in trust and sincerity to seek answers and find healing through Christ. It takes the Holy Spirit to do the work of healing. The Holy Spirit is 'he' that is pleased or offended and not mankind. The trusting and sincere will never offend the Divine but the proud and presumptuous do. Therefore all whom the spirit of God will heal must be sincere and trust as obedient children do.

The spirit within the faithful matured in Christ never sleeps but remains awake at all hours night and day. The flesh oftentimes hinders the work of the spirit. Therefore the spirit is most effectual at night when the flesh is asleep and out of the way. Evil works flourish in the darkness of the night times. This is when the spirit of God is used by the heavenly Father to break the cords of bondage in answer to prayers. It is therefore important that prayers be offered to God without ceasing for every child at night before bedtime. The spirit of the Father works through the bearer of light at night when the forces of evil are at work. Evil exposed to the true light of Christ vacates those places where it has found a home. God remains unseen by the eyes of man but he can be perceived where the true light of Christ has risen in the heart to serve his will on earth. All who bear true light can 'see' God and are equipped to bring down the works of evil wherever encountered. Such that bear Truth in the light of Christ can take evil captive and cast it away where it can do little or no harm.

The bearer of light is a calf that has been reared to maturity in the stall of the Almighty Father. He is a sacred cow who exists for the meat of the spirit within and not for the meat of his flesh. It takes many seasons, at least seventeen years or more, to grow into full spiritual maturity in Christ and to be deemed righteous before God. The faithful that is matured in Christ has grown from grace as child to stand before God as a man under mercy. Christ has brought him home to be adopted by the heavenly Father into the family with a new name. The adopted has escaped death to become timeless for his spirit will live forever. Therefore he must devote his time on earth to do the heavenly Father's bidding above all things. Seventeen years is a long time to tarry for God but it is the blink of an eye in the scope of eternity. Eternity is creation's grand blessing and the golden crown of life. It is hard to let go of fame and fortune when one does not yet know that those two are impostors. Fame and fortune are rewards at best but blessings are far better for they never cease. Blessings never come with regrets and are passed forward to the next generation. Such are good everywhere and anytime. Eternal life and divine blessings, whoever has those can have anything that his heart desires.

Righteousness before God is not realized by the laws of Moses. The commandments of Moses are rudimentary laws which the believer can start with. The laws serve well to help mankind lead a moral and ethical life but to his surprise he will often find himself failing in one aspect of it or another. Obedience to the laws of Moses does not make man righteous. Righteousness before God is a far different matter. It pertains to those things that God wants the believer to do or not do. The secrets of the kingdom of God are communicated when the inner man is ready. As one matures in Christ, he is made aware of certain secrets of the kingdom so that he can be righteous before God.

Christ Jesus kept certain truths hidden from the masses but revealed them in private to the chosen. The secret things belong to God but those secrets communicated in spirit are done so that the faithful can remain obedient to the laws of God. Those are the statutes by which he will be shielded from the evil and corruption that surrounds him in the world. The faithful in light has to be shielded so that he can remain a clean vessel into which the father can pour a 'potion' of himself as the need arises. He who knows to observe the statutes appointed to him soon becomes the righteous in covenant with God. He will abide in the secret place of the Almighty God to remain in an everlasting covenant. Such has become a son of Heaven that can never be separated from the love of God.

Every son of the covenant has persevered in his spiritual journey to have Christ come to full spiritual maturity within him. He has become justified before God as well to be bestowed with righteousness. It is an exalted honor and he who is so blessed must not be ashamed to declare it. It is not self that the righteous declares but Christ within him. Unless the lamp is placed on a stand, many will not receive the benefits of its light. The declaration of Christ within is affirmed as God uses the son of covenant to answer the prayers of many. Everyone so exalted has been elected to serve a flock appointed for him within an earthly plot. The son of covenant lives a life of amazement but first he has to pass through the crucible of the world's rejection so that he can learn to remain humble. He is often persecuted for love of Truth and for walking on the path that pleases God and not men. He has to pass through the fire of the world's hatred before he can be baptized in spirit to be welcomed into the secret place.

The son of covenant lives as an instrument to receive from God through Christ and share with the willing so that his will is carried out on earth. The spirit of the enemy acts in disobedience to the will of God. But the spirit of Christ acts in obedience to his sovereign will. When the spirit of God speaks to the heart the faithful must obey for evil not to overwhelm humanity. It is righteousness fulfilled when mankind obeys God in all things and at all times. The power to destroy the works of evil on earth wherever such exist is the birthright of the sons. That birthright is the trump card that assures victory for them through Christ.

Chapter Highlights

- ✓ The enemy is a determined foe who aims for the spiritual strangulation of mankind's offspring.
- ✓ The enemy aims to corrupt the children so that mankind's future is bound with him in the earthen.
- ✓ Mankind can never reconnect with God as long as he is determined to do it in his mind and flesh.
- ✓ The earth is recycled for the worthy to be salvaged so that the unworthy is burnt in a fire of judgment.
- ✓ The heavenly Father searches everything on earth so that nothing redeemable or salvageable is lost.
- ✓ The gifts received from above uplift man's soul and satisfy his longings for fulfillment and peace.
- ✓ The enemy is rendered powerless and shamed into oblivion when he is withstood by true light.
- ✓ The 'child' that looks in the mirror of Truth will receive insight into the man he is ordained to be.
- ✓ Though the heavenly Father remains unseen he can be perceived in the faithful who serve his will.
- ✓ God's elect is a sacred cow who exists for the meat of the spirit and not for the meat of his flesh.
- ✓ The faithful that remains a clean vessel will always be filled with a 'potion' of the divine.
- ✓ He that is privy to Divine will but acts not on it unwittingly serves the purposes of the enemy.
- ✓ The power to destroy evil wherever encountered is the birthright of the sons.

The voice of Truth echoes in love

Through every color and tongue

So mankind can know the Divine

Regardless of guise HE appears in

Chapter 18

OF TRUTH, LIGHT AND LOVE

God desires nothing more than to be in spiritual communion with his favorite creation man. Sadly man's sinful ways and pride make this communal fellowship with God impossible. Mankind needs to understand that his reconciliation with the heavenly Father rests on two unchangeable truths. Firstly, he must accept that all have sinned and come short of the glory of God. Secondly, he has to confess his sins and accept the sacrifice availed by grace through Christ as payment for sin in order to be reconciled with God. Though it sounds simple enough, yet mankind willfully refuses to accept the gift of grace readily. It is in man's nature to expect punishment and reprisal for every offence committed. He fails to recognize or accept that the sin nature is one area where he is powerless to do anything. He is powerless because spiritual payment is required to cleanse man of sin. Sinful man is not able to make this payment because he is spiritually dead. Yet he cannot become spiritually alive until payment is made.

Someone acceptable to God as a suitable sacrifice has to

make the spiritual payment in man's stead so that his dead spirit can awaken to life. The gift of new life is the noblest of all gifts and man can receive it through Christ. Christ Jesus has made the payment for sin so that all who believe in him as mankind's redeemer can have a chance of reconciliation with God. For true believers, the spirit within can be awakened to new life if that is the Divine will for such. God who searches the hearts of mankind knows their contents and intentions. God is the final arbiter and chooses whom he deems fit for awakening within to begin the journey of spiritual transformation that leads to him.

In order to walk faithfully on the path towards God, the awakened in spirit must continue to feed and live in accordance with Truth. Living in obedience to Truth helps to sustain the awakened spirit in the way of light on to full maturity in Christ. Living in the light of Truth through the teachings of Christ affords the divine essence to inspire and strengthen the spirit within the believer. The word of God that he feeds upon is the bread of life that will in time turn into spiritual meat within the believer as he matures in the way of light after Christ. It is for this reason that it is important for the believer to devote quality time to prayer and study of the word of Truth. The hour of prayer is the refueling stop for the spirit. It is the water break taken at the oasis of life by the weary traveler. The believer must drink regularly from the trough of the living water of the word else his nascent spirit will die of thirst. The young spirit, like all growing entities, must be regularly fed.

A more than necessary or inordinate focus on the things of the world is a great trap for many who seek after God. The hunger for earthly materials is a great inhibitor of man's spirit and faith in God. The love of the things of the world results in the neglect and rejection of God's way of light. The way of God and that of the world are opposed to each other. There will never be compromise between the two. God is faithful but very jealous. He leaves man with the choice to follow the way his heart desires. It is this choice determined solely by the desires and intentions of each man's heart that prescribes the spiritual path that he will take in life. For many the door to the heavenly Father will forever remain closed. But for some it will always be open to receive due welcome into his family because their hearts seek after righteousness.

Those who love Truth and seek after righteousness will be availed the light of God to direct their footsteps. They will be guided in that light to follow after Christ and will meet him in due season in accordance with God's will. God always makes accommodation for the spiritually ignorant to find redemption. For this reason, his Spirit will induce the man availed light to share with others in love so that such can begin to perceive as he does. The sight received in light is spiritual perception and it is a gift from the heavenly Father to some but not to all men. Many in the world lack this spiritual gift and so cast about oblivious of the Divine. They lack spiritual sight because they let the dictates of the world be the guide of their life. They that lack perception often regress into outer darkness where hopelessness abound and the dead or dying dwell.

The gift of spiritual sight is a very special gift. It is not to be taken lightly but must be cherished and treasured in the heart. He who has this gift is able to see the pitfalls and entrapments that the prince of darkness has dug all over the world. Spiritual sight is like a navigational instrument to guide the footsteps and aid the faithful believer in his earthly journey. The world is an obstacle course which must be navigated successfully to win the crown of eternal life reserved for the worthy by God. All start the race but only those guided in light and shielded in love by the unseen hand of God are successful at the end.

The prince of darkness has dug all manner of traps in his determination to stop as many as he can from completing the obstacle course of the world in victory. God on the other hand provides necessary navigational instruments and guidance tools to aid the faithful to complete the course. He waits anxiously and in earnest expectation for those appointed for victory in this light. He already knows how many will complete the course and so he spares no efforts to make sure that they do. The obstacle course of the world is definitely a maze but the eyes of God are always on the faithful to avail them light to direct their footsteps. And so every faithful believer whose eyes and heart are fixed on God will always be guided in true light.

Those deemed worthy by God are marked by a common

attribute. They are compassionate of heart and do not withhold mercy from the needy. Much has been given to them and the Father expects much in return from them. They have been prepared and equipped to act as the Father would if he were here on earth himself. The faithful believer that is used by God to carry out his will on earth is a divine proxy. He who has been chosen in this wise must open his heart to all for he has become a conduit for divine help to reach mankind and for goodness to abound. Such is one filled with essence of the Divine and must not shut off the stream of benevolence from flowing through him.

As the faithful fulfills his role and lives in accordance to Truth with love for God, he will be infused with the attributes of the Divine. He that has been infused with godly attributes can induce those same attributes or essence in all that sincerely embrace Truth. The godly in spirit can help seekers find healing and obtain release from the things that trouble them. They are God's anointed physicians, in the same wise as Christ Jesus, in that through them many will come to find answers for life's ailments. They that are endued with godly attributes are enthroned in grace and therefore have access into the preserve of the mercy wherein mankind's needs are met by the heavenly Father.

The faithful believer that has access into the preserve of mercy has been exalted into the place where all wishes are duly granted. The preserve of mercy is where all that are needed by the faithful are provided. It is the dispensary where the physician makes requisition for all that he needs to help make people and situations whole. Every physician in this wise has received the gift of insight and will be divinely endued with wisdom as needed. Such is exalted and will not see things as most men do but perceive from a higher plane. He sees from above and will therefore be circumspective in all matters. The circumspective in spirit is able to know what is needed, lacking or cluttering the way and can sort things out to make them better.

He that God has deemed to be worthy must use his gifts well and complete the mission ordained for him as the time is limited. Often the ordained mission is a lifelong calling and involves much sacrifice but God knows that. Therefore he has set a season for every faithful servant to come into faith rest after such has honored his calling. The burden of Christ does come to an end when the worthy before God have raised others worthy to serve God in light. It is all in accordance with God's will and mankind has no say in the matter. Being that the season appointed for those that serve God under the burden of Christ is limited, such must labor diligently to serve him well as the good shepherds appointed for the flock.

All who are not in fellowship with Christ are outside the will of God and in league with the prince of darkness. There is no neutrality in the battle of light against darkness for it has to be one or the other. The love of the world has blinded the faithless so that they have given room for darkness to thrive in their lives. In their willful blindness, such have led the unwary into the ditches of sin. The unwitting victims of sin have to be led back to the path of righteousness for God will not suffer the souls of those whom he has earmarked for redemption and predestined for salvation to suffer corruption. Every one unwittingly led into sin is appointed a 'savior' to come to his rescue in the light of Christ and only to such will the lost respond.

The Spirit that calls in love from within those matured in Christ is one that all those predestined for salvation had known from a long time ago in their distant past. It is the call of destiny that echoes ceaselessly and timelessly in the hearts of all who will come to be reconciled with God. Such are destined for spiritual transformation to become adopted into the divine household. They are led to pass through certain places, encounter certain people and do certain things during their earthly sojourn. It is at the meeting points of these places, people and things that the enemy has laid his traps of deception. It is at these entrapment points that the faith of the believer is tested and victory is wrought. It has all been programmed from the beginning of time by the heavenly Father.

Truth will always guide the faithful believer who has put his trust in God past every obstacle in his way through the light of Christ. Ways of escape will be availed to him to escape temptations as well as be shielded from the evil ploys of the enemy. He that has been so shielded and guided through Christ is called to be the guide to bring others from the darkness into light. He must respond to this calling for it is by such that he will come to know and be known in Heaven above as well as on earth below. He who responds well and is productive in this calling will be ushered deeper into the wellspring of the Divine. He will be the faithful laborer granted access into the purer and truer to duly realize the fullness of the riches of God.

The realm of the pure and true is the place of victorious living where God makes many miracles to come about. He that has tasted the pure and true will never be content with the glory that the world affords. He may have a taste of it but he will find the worldly to be unfulfilling and dissatisfactory. True fulfillment can only be realized in the fullness of time as the faithful fulfills the mission divinely destined for him through Christ. It is in the harvest field of Christ that the Father imparts his glory on the faithful for worthy service. Therefore the true laborer must get on with the task before him as the time appointed is limited. He that has been bestowed with divine glory is a son of light anointed to help true seekers after Christ realize hope of eternal life with the heavenly Father.

Whatever the son of light encounters along the way in his earthly path is foreknown. God therefore makes provision so he can be availed that needed to overcome problems and obstacles. Every son of light has three silver bullets given to him to handle the issues of life. His thoughts and wishes are like bullets that stream out to heavenly places to connect with the Father, the first born Son Jesus as well as the Spirit. They are used to summon help and to accomplish the desires of the heart. The christened will not comprehend the depth of that which has been poured into him initially. But he will come to understand the extent of the power that he is connected to as he passes through and overcomes many problems. The sharpness of every sword is only understood and appreciated by the many beasts slain with it on life's path. The words that the follower in light after Christ speaks constitute the sword. The silver bullets are only entrusted to those who have wielded the sword nobly. He that has the silver bullet need not speak much anymore for as he thinks in his heart, so it comes to pass. Yet he may not fully understand that he has come into unity with God whose wisdom is unsearchable and depths unfathomable. And so, he only scratches the surface of what is possible within the divine infinitude.

Every son of light will never encounter more than he can handle. Every trial that encounters is to show him a little more of what is possible through the heavenly Father. He that reaches out for more will find the light to get brighter and brighter. The temptations may get more challenging but every son has been given the Holy Ghost to inform him and the Holy Spirit to enable him in all things. God always accompanies the sons through life in truth, light and love.

It is companionship framed with goodness and mercy in abiding faith where the Father can never leave the son and nothing can separate from the eternity of divine love.

It is a promise made by the heavenly Father in love that his anointing will be with the faithful in goodness and mercy. He that has the anointing of the Divine will always be refreshed in light. The believer that faithfully walks in the light of Christ will always find refreshment even as he pours out himself in love to all who embrace Truth. When truth and light lead into the love that never ceases, life becomes glorified. Where life has becomes glorified, death is vanquished. For the faithful that have been found worthy by God, death is no longer the end of life's journey but the continuation of a glorious life in divine love. Glory belongs to God and things become glorified when he plays a decisive role in them. Such is what defines eternity for it is that realm where life is glorified through the warmth of love, light of Christ and power of God so death has no stake there. It is to join up with the Divine in the forever glory of eternity that the faithful labor and hope for.

Chapter Highlights

- ✓ New life is a noble gift and mankind can receive such in love through the light of Christ.
- ✓ Truth affords the divine essence that the inner man draws inspiration and strength from.
- ✓ He who lets the dictates of the world be the guide of life will be blind and lack spiritual perception.
- ✓ Spiritual perception guides the footsteps of the faithful believer in his earthly journey through life.
- ✓ The faithful guided by the Divine is able to find his way through the maze of the world in victory.
- ✓ The compassionate and charitable are chosen by God to be conduits for divine gifts to the needy.
- ✓ The essence of divine living is manifested in things that are fulfilling, sustainable and enduring.
- ✓ The exalted in light know what is important or cluttering the way in any given situation.
- ✓ It is at the entrapment points laid down by the enemy that faith is tested and victory wrought.
- ✓ The faithful that is productive in his calling is ushered deeper into the wellspring of the Divine.
- ✓ Glory belongs to God and things become glorified when he plays a role in earthly endeavors.

Christ is 'compassion' by one for another

Man that has same honors a divine wish

For each man that is his brother's keeper

Obeys that command dear to God's heart

Chapter 19

THE FAITHFUL ARE BLESSED

Every son of light is a vehicle of goodness and mercy that has been implanted with divine seeds by the heavenly Father on behalf of humanity. God entrusts such precious seeds to the sons in the hope that they will use their time and energy on earth to plant as well as nurture that implanted in their hearts. God sends help as needed and gives the increase but each son must plant the seed entrusted to him. The precious is perceived in light by the sons within the field of dreams where immortal souls re-create in love as led by the spirit of goodness and mercy. Every partaker in this greater light must have strong faith for it is the means to realize that seen in figures. God who shows the dream in goodness also makes the necessary arrangements and pre-positions everything in mercy that will be needed to make it come about.

Each son must plant and bring the seed that the Father has entrusted to him to full life. He is called to graft his wishes on to the tree of life so that the desired fruit can be harvested therefrom. God dotes on the sons of light on account of their love of Truth. He uses them as his earthly proxies in the battle of truth against evil, light against darkness, love over hatred and life over death. The sons bear true testament in greater light through Christ to uplift humanity's soul and are inspired to accomplish many 'great' works in God's name for his hand is always with them. The greatness of the works that they do is not reckoned by the grandeur but by purity of intention and purpose. Such are works that shine before men to lead them to praise and give due glory to God for his goodness.

Each son of light cannot help but produce good fruits for he carries anointed seeds. The handiworks borne of the anointed endure for God initiates and brings them to fruition. Such works may not be imposing or overwhelm the senses. They may even appear little in the eyes of mankind. But such is the seed of Ephraim, the little one that is much beloved by the Father. He who bears the anointed seed must maintain it in good custody. His motivation must remain pure for he has been called to accomplish works that bring God due glory. He will rebuild the broken down, lift up the down trodden and give voice to the inaudible as God speaks through him. Only in that wise are the faithful accounted as part of the building block of God's kingdom of light.

He that has become part of the kingdom of light must cease from casting the precious to swindling folk for what he has received from the Divine must be treasured. That which he has received must be held in good custody for those willing to embrace Truth in the light of Christ. It takes the divinely anointed seed to bear the fruit of the vine that produces the new wine of regeneration through Christ. Only the faithful that seek after Christ in true light and not for gain can receive the new wine. Many will not be able to receive or see value in that which is availed in divine light for it is veiled to them to know. There is a veil and dimness of soul that must be lifted from mankind before he is able to perceive the things of the Divine. It is up to God to lift that veil from man's soul for only he can determine the hearts that are worthy. Regeneration serves to replenish the empty, restore the dying and bring out the new from the demise of the old. Regeneration is availed by God in goodness and mercy. It is a gift that validates the journey of spiritual transformation in that only the matured in Christ can afford it.

Every son of light is a universal spirit who has been adopted into the family of the heavenly Father. He sees all men as his brothers for he knows that God is the Creator of all. He is called in spirit to model his life so that others can learn the heavenly way that leads the lost back home to the Father of all. He is also a good custodian of nature and knows not to desecrate the goodness in creation. Each son understands that he is just passing through the earth to a heavenly and better home. Therefore he looks not to sit pretty on earth for he knows that he has not arrived at his destined home yet. His spirit knows of a better place beyond the walls of man's flesh. And so his days on earth amount to a dress rehearsal for the better life that he has glimpsed. He lives filled with the hope of that which awaits him after his work on earth is done and is guided to live in the spirit of universal brotherhood that applies wherever divine will reign supreme. It makes no difference whether here on earth or in the exalted realm beyond he has become a good citizen of the universal kingdom of light.

Most followers of Christ only have experience of the two dimensions of the Holy Trinity. They have experience of the spirit without which no one can respond to the conscience. They also have experience of the son or the embodiment of Truth without which no one can begin the journey of spiritual transformation. The believer that has experience of the two dimensions of the Trinity is not fully matured in Spirit. He is still lacks experience of the Father and will be precluded from knowing his will. Those that have experience of two dimensions of the Divine serve God in lesser light but cannot serve him in greater light as the sons can. The believer that has experience of the two dimensions of the Trinity will be of profitable service on earth as a minister of the gospel. But he can only provide the milk of the word of Truth and not the meat. He can be no more than that for the veiled will be hidden from him.

The fully matured in light has experience of the three dimensions of the Divine. Such is a son of God even as

Christ Jesus the first born in light is. Every son of light is an apostle of the faith chosen to be a lamb of sacrifice for those that he shepherds in the way of Christ. He is the one who carries the cross for those who flock to him in that he has laid his life down for them. He will pass through the darkness of rejection and the world's hatred into the light of ascension as a son of Heaven beloved by the Father. This is a very special calling for a select number whom God has chosen from the foundation of time to predestine their life's path on earth. The profile of their life mirrors that of Christ Jesus and only they can truly understand his most arcane teachings. They are all woven from the same fabric of the golden threads of life which the heavenly Father himself spins. Such are the ones who are remade in the likeness of the Father and are able to eat meat with the divinely appointed. The eaters of the meat of the word are given knowledge of key words to make victory possible in all things and in every endeavor. They are custodians of such mysteries of the kingdom of light steeped in the pure dew of Truth and distilled from the mists of time.

The collective memory of all things that have gone before is divinely encoded in the consciousness of the sons of light so that they can show mankind how he can cease from stumbling back to the past that haunts him so. The sons are also endued with prescient knowledge borne of the Holy Ghost from the heavenly throne so that they can show the way that will lead humanity to salvation and dawn in a better future that will glorify mankind. They are the householders who out of the treasure chests of their hearts bring out things that are new but old. Such congregate spiritually around the hub of creation and are therefore able to re-create things to make them better. He that eats the meat of the word has arrived at the top of God's mountain but he is called to come down to the valley to share wisdom with those that lack. He must come down to the valley where many flounder spiritually to share those things that God has entrusted to him. He has become one that no longer seeks his own gain in the world but lives for the welfare of humanity as all are kindred folk of the same heavenly Father. It is by living to make others whole that the sons are forever reborn in the timelessness of divine light to make their souls immortal. They know that nothing done for goodness sake to please God is ever wasted for the heavenly Father unfailingly repays such endeavors with the good and perfect.

There are seasons appointed when the power of God is accessible to the seeker. This is when God is near and can be found easily by those who seek after him in true light. When the appointed season passes by, it becomes much more difficult to connect spiritually with the Divine. There is a season in the affairs of men when fortune's tide rises for them and the divine wind strives with them. It is too much of a risk for man to put away till tomorrow that which he can do today that might bring him nearer to God. In as much as salvation is by God's will, man must take the necessary first steps towards him so that he may be ascertained of his place within the Divine fold.

Many in the world have already let the season appointed for them to connect with the Divine pass by. There were occasions in their lives when God availed his grace to them in the hope that their hearts will be turned towards him. In that appointed season, the message of the gospel of Truth was shared with them in love but they rejected such. In an effort to change their hardened hearts, God answered prayers for them, showed the face of Providence and extended the hand of Benevolence to them but to no avail. They refused to let in the power of God in their lives when it was near to heal and redeem them. And so, it is by such hard heartedness that many have remained unable to escape from the darkening veil of worldliness to continue to live with a blanket over their spiritual eyes.

The spiritually blind live under the false assumption that righteousness is about the works of man's hand and so labor for such that men fawn over. Such have falsely concluded that righteousness is about appearances instead of the purity of the heart. And so they choose to seek after the praise of men and earthly glory through such works. Man's undertakings are of no interest to God if not carried out in accordance with his divine will. It is obedience to his will that really counts with God and makes man righteous before him. He often asks man to do that thing or follow that way which may appear befuddling to him in his limited understanding and finite knowledge.

To obey God's will is always better than man's pretentious sacrifices. Quite to his surprise, man is often amazed at the outcomes in those times when he allows the will of God to guide him in life. Nevertheless whether man likes it or not, God's will is sovereign and always prevail in the end.

It takes grace to accept God's will as sovereign in good faith and for mankind to dedicate every endeavor to God. Grace is that which one gives and shares with another in love through Christ. It flows in love from the Divine through the saintly in spirit to the newest member within the body of Christ. It is the undercurrent that moves along the body and allows for the spread the kingdom of light. The fellowship or body of Christ is a communion of spirits in a common faith to serve the will of God in love. It is a commonwealth where one lives for all and all live for one in allegiance to God by goodness and mercy.

There are some things that the believer is not able to do or have access to when he is young in faith. However he will not lack those things for such needs will be provided for him by others through grace. As he grows in faith he will then have the ability to get and do those things for himself. He will no longer need grace in those areas where he has become capable. There is therefore a point when the window of grace is closed and the door of mercy is opened for the worthy. The unwise who takes the feast of grace through Christ for granted by hoarding, taking undue advantage and not being duly thankful to God will be left out of the divine will. He will not have the door of mercy opened for him when the window of mercy is closed. Such is a false confessor who takes the name of Christ in vain by failing to partake worthily of grace which he has received freely in the way. By his disobedience, selfishness and vanity, he is repeatedly subjecting his fellow believers to unnecessary hardship and crucifying the body of Christ.

The unworthy partaker of grace commits the sin of 'Caan' in not being a keeper of his brother in good faith. Each believer within the fellowship of Christ is his brother's keeper called to uplift the other in light of love. It is for this reason that Christ Jesus always paired the disciples in twos so that each can provide the other with what he lacks. Simon Peter who hears the inaudible voice is always paired with Andrew who is courageous. It is a good thing to know God's will but it takes the brave hearted to obey it. In the same vein, James or one who does something new is paired with John or one who is gracious. The way of light through Christ is only made possible and established in grace. One believer helps to meet the lack of another within the apportionment of grace. It is love of the world and its passing glory that leads the faithless to commit the sin of 'Caan'. It is in so doing that mankind is spiritually estranged from God and knowledge of his will. He that is estranged from the Divine is left to dwell in the shadowy and dark places of the world to seek after one transient glory after another with no fulfillment there to be found.

Every son of light will always abide in spirit for he has come into an eternal habitation with God. The hardships of the world may hurt his flesh but his spirit will remain untouchable by the world. Such knows the pure and true for his spirit has ascended up the mountain of God to be sanctified and embalmed in Truth. His flesh may abide in the valley but his spirit can ascend up God's holy mountain to soak up the essence of the Divine. Yet the spirit that ascends up there must return to the valley to shine light so the spiritually blind can come into true knowledge. He that can ascend up the holy mountain is used to do the amazing before man to God's glory. Such that can ascend to the pure and true is a cloud borne of the Divine to bring needed rain to dry and desert places so that the famished can be refreshed to bloom again.

They that have been to the mountain top cannot help those who are manipulative, seeks after self-glory or engages in pursuits that will grieve the Spirit of God. They cannot help the abusers of grace for such have the gift of the Holy Ghost who affords them knowledge of the secret and hidden things. They that return to the valley come to enrich and bring about needed change so goodness can abound in light and love. They return to bring knowledge and wisdom from the heavenly down to earthly places so that many may share in the priceless availed in love by God to mankind through the light of Christ.

Chapter Highlights

- ✓ Works of glory result from that which is revealed in divine light and perceived with eyes of the spirit.
- ✓ Works of glory are not reckoned with worldly measures but shine due to purity of purpose.
- ✓ The handiworks of the elect endure for God initiates and brings them to fruition.
- ✓ Regeneration validates spiritual transformation and affords mankind the means for works of glory.
- ✓ The faithful do not look to sit pretty on earth for they know that they have not arrived home yet.
- ✓ The sons of God share the profile of Christ and are woven from the fabric of everlasting life.
- ✓ In seeking to make others worthy in light, the sons are reborn in a timeless and eternal cycle.
- ✓ The faithless that yield not to divine will stumble in the world for they will have a blanket over the eye.
- ✓ The believer will always be amazed at the outcome when he yields to the divine sovereign will.
- ✓ The body of Christ is a commonwealth where all pledge allegiance to God in Truth, light and love.
- ✓ The believer that will not lift up his brother in kindness is bound to dwell in darkness.
- ✓ He that is matured in Christ will remain untouched in spirit by that which may hurt his flesh.
- ✓ The abusers of grace are precluded from the good gifts divinely availed under mercy.

Man anointed to be harbinger of the new

And break the chain of human mediocrity

Must go beyond the bounds of the known

For thereabouts is glory ordained for him

Chapter 20

AN EXALTED VIEW

Every one reborn in divine light is able to see earthly things from a heavenly perspective. The spirit that dwells within the reborn may be likened to the eagle that has mastered the rigors of flight despite the challenges encountered along the way. The eagle-in-spirit can soar to the heavenly heights there to have the clarity of vision availed only 'above the cloudy'. The spirit of the reborn can soar to the abode of the stars that men are wistful of and dream about. That abode is the playing field of the immortal souls from where re-creation is carried out. From that starry height, the reborn has a unique view on how to possess that which he desires on earth. It is this unique view that enables him to make the amazing happen on earth even though he may appear little in the eyes of the worldly.

It is this vantage point that Christ Jesus refers to when he speaks about overcoming the world. The faithful believer is able to scale the starry heights and come into the greater light availed thereabouts through the embrace of Truth and obedience to God's will. He who perseveres in the love of Truth through Christ will be duly exalted into greater light in accordance with the Father's will. He will come to commune in spirit with God and to become an embodiment of Truth as well as a beacon of light who will put the heavenly Father's business above all else.

There is the issue of the passion of Christ which the seeker must go through in order to reach the greater heights. The latter being the highest peak in the mountain of faith can only be scaled by those chosen to do so by the Father. Ascending that peak is a test of faith that demands love for Christ and total trust in God's faithfulness to deliver as promised. There is a ledge two-thirds up the mountain where most seekers after Christ settle to go no further. Those who go beyond the ledge to reach summit of faith become reborn in divine light for they have overcome the world. The mountain summit is Heaven's tableland where the table has been laid out for the faithful. Those that are able to ascend to the summit become privy to divine will to be duly used as agents for recreating the valley below in the order of heaven above. Such get their marching orders from the heavenly heights but come down to the valley to do the work ordained for them by the Father.

They that make it to the summit of the mountain return to the valley as changed men with a better vision and deeper understanding of God. Sadly many are spiritually blind and cannot perceive those that have ascended the summit. They are often viewed as misguided purveyors of strange doctrines and therefore many will not entertain or embrace the Truth that they share. Mankind always tends to reject the 'new wine' initially for it is unfamiliar to the palate until he can acquire the taste for it. Be that as it may, those given to embrace the 'new wine' availed in greater light will do so and come to be immensely blessed. The reborn in light may seem otherwise but are indeed emissaries of the heavenly Father sent to the spiritually blind. They are the closest that men will come to see God who has infused them with many of his divine attributes.

Many misguidedly reject those reborn in divine light for they do not look the part when judged with human eyes. Man looks on the outside but God who seeks after the heart looks inward. He seeks after the hearts that are compassionate and merciful. Such are those who feel the pain of others and are ready to forgive in love for they know that God forgives them in kind. The compassionate and merciful fit the mold of Christ and are invariably deemed righteous by God to stand before him in mercy. By embracing Truth, such have let the light and love of Christ to abound as well as reach many on earth.

The passion of Christ, though it is heavy tribulation for man's flesh is necessary for spiritual transformation and transcendence. It is the process that every true seeker after Christ has to pass through so that he can shed the 'weight' of the worldly that encumbers the spirit. It is by this rigorous sacrifice that the muscle of the spirit is toned and the flesh tamed so that a more streamlined inner person may emerge. He who is on a pilgrimage to meet up with Christ has no need for much of the worldly that men crave. The things that a man craves possess his soul and are the tentacles that keep him tethered to the worldly. The passion endured in the way after Christ affords the believer the means to let go of those things that keep his spirit earthbound. It serves as the catharsis by which the seeker is purified from inside out. It is passion that lays a heavy burden on man's soul but it serves to squeeze out the last residue and vestiges of darkness that still hides in the heart. The passion endured in the way after Christ brings suffering and hurting in the flesh. Yet it not only serves to purify the spirit but also serves to open the door for those chosen to join God's divine family.

In an ironic twist, the only way for mankind to satisfy his hunger for the glory of the world is for his old self with its ego to be buried in dust. In order to escape from the tentacles that bind him to earth, man must bury his old nature in the dirt of the earth so that it may have its fill of dust. Man's worst enemy is his ego but his best friend is the little spark of the divine that God has left in every man. Unless his ego is buried in the dirt of the earth, the best in man cannot be free to come forth. The essence of the glory of the world is nothing but dust. Man cannot build on it for it is soon scattered by the winds to be forgotten in the mists of time. The glory of earth's dust blinds man's spiritual eyes and suffocates his mind. It is the bed of the prideful and self-glorified in which the serpent, that is the enemy of all things godly, makes his home. It is only by the way of Christ that man can cast pride aside and leave all his self-glorifying tendencies behind.

The man that has cast pride aside to seek after God in humility will in due season become exalted as a son of light if it is divinely appointed for him. In order to become a son, the seeker must follow after the footsteps of Christ Jesus. The journey of spiritual transformation is the same and the experiences similar. The chastisement is the same for all destined to become sons certain in God. The testing points of faith are the same and it is thereabouts that every believer has to be proven worthy. In order to become certain in God, the believer must live through certain experiences, pass through certain places and encounter certain people. The temptations are the same as well as the rewards. The latter day sons of the Father must do in their own times even as the sons of earlier times did in theirs. It is by overcoming temptations at the testing points of faith that the believer is availed strong faith and great vision needed to achieve the glorious.

The days of the power of God are those moments when divine will intersects with space and time to do the miraculous on earth. It is on those days that the Spirit of God moves the sons to do the amazing before mankind. It is for those moments that the faithful tarry. It is like wind-gliding or sail-surfing when the unseen hand of nature lifts the adventurous to take flight effortlessly. The sons of light venture forth on such occasions on spiritual wings to serve God's purposes in faith. The Father will do the same for every worthy son as he did for Christ Jesus for they are all kindred in spirit. Christ is the same yesterday, today and forever. What one son knows others can know and what one has the others can have too as sons of one Father with same rights and privileges under divine mercy.

Mankind loses the use of his spiritual wings when he emerges from his mother's womb into the world. He loses his spiritual wings when he begins to see with the eyes and live by the dictates of the world around him. Therefore as time passes by mankind becomes a spiritually deficient entity that is a moribund earth-dweller and bottom-feeder within the divine order. The moribund is a blind and egocentric anomaly that has no portion with the Divine. Such has to be replaced by a new inner man that is selfless through the light of Christ before man can regain his sight and spiritual wings. The new self that emerges after the ego has been buried in dust is remade to soar in spirit. The reborn in spirit soon rediscovers his wings and learns to use them again through the light of Christ. The reborn in light can see with the eye of the spirit to know that the heavenly is distinct from the earthly. Such is one that becomes a 'hybrid' being who alternates between the heavenly heights above and the earthly below. He is a gentleman or gentle giant whose mind touches the sky. He is able to rub off of the lamp of divine genius to bring enlightenment to earth so that the cause of light over darkness may be advanced. He is the true and noble that has said no to the dust of the world's glory. In saying no to the world's way, he has yes to Christ to become a noble son of righteousness and a trustee in the heavenly Father's business on earth. He has become a confidant of the Divine in the important matters that concern mankind.

The heavenly Father is a God of purpose and has a plan for everyone and all things in his creation. Everything in creation has a destined purpose whether estimated to be good or bad by mankind. It has to be so because God does not want, haste or waste. His plans are all encompassing and lead into the future of eternity. As the present age runs out its due course and the new age looms, the workings of the hand of God are coalescing into an ever evolving grand mosaic. He that is able to see the grand picture ceases from stumbling around in his own pursuits but settles into a purpose-driven life dictated by the evolving picture that he 'sees'. He that can see soon enters into an easing of spirit and into the peace that passes understanding. He that is in such a state begins to have a fuller and more complete understanding of the mind of God for he has become joined to the divine will. It is a sort of time lapse photography that displays certain imminent and future events that the mindful in Christ are able to process in the light of Truth. They can 'see' because their inner eyes have been fully opened through faith to glimpse from the past all the way into the future.

He that has come into God's peace and an easing of spirit is accompanied by an aura of hopeful glow. It is a brilliant glow exuded when the spirit within is at peace with the Divine. It is a glow perceived by all but which the faithless cannot fathom. The faithless who has tied his fate to that of the world cannot fathom things concerning the Divine. Love of the world estranges such from God and results in the aborting of divine plans. It is man's unceasing wants for the things of the world that blinds and aborts God's plans for him. It shrouds his soul in dimness and plagues him with nagging dissatisfaction and emptiness.

Christ is compassionate and merciful. He gives in selfless sacrifice that bears faithful testimony to divine goodness and mercy. Christ receives from God and gives to others without asking for anything in return except to remind man to love and honor the Creator. All that Christ says and does may not be pleasing to man at first but will bring him goodness later. The new way may take getting used to but the merits and benefits of the light of Christ are revealed in the passage of time. Time exposes both Christ and the prince of darkness for who they are. Christ is a giver of good and perfect gifts who forgives in mercy. But the prince of the darkness is an accuser who seeks after the damnation of all that is good and perfect before God.

Chapter Highlights

- ✓ The exalted spiritual height is the realm where the faithful believer comes to overcome the world.
- ✓ The exalted realm changes mankind as it offers a clearer and deeper understanding of God.
- ✓ Many have forgone their blessings through judging by looks instead of by the heart and light of Truth.
- ✓ The suffering endured in Christ affords the means for the catharsis that purifies from the inside out.
- ✓ The glory of the world is dust that the wise that seeks after eternal things cannot build on.
- ✓ The walk of faith leads the believer through certain times and places to have certain experiences.
- ✓ Days of divine power are times when divine will converges with space and time to do the amazing.
- ✓ Mankind begins to lose his spiritual wings when he emerges from the maternal womb into the world.
- ✓ God has an all-encompassing plan for everything and everyone in creation.
- ✓ The believer that comes into an assured peace has an aura of hope that is unmistakable.
- ✓ He who refuses to embrace Truth will forfeit the chance to be cloaked with the garment of eternity.
- ✓ All that the Christ says and does may not be pleasing to man at first but it brings goodness later.

An ordained and purposed life awaits him

Whose soul is washed and purified in Truth

A place in congregation of the living is his

As one deemed worthy to serve the Divine

Books for Spiritual Guidance by Kalu Onwuka

Nuggets of Resurrection is an engaging discourse that explores the many gifts available to the spiritually matured in Christ, the path that seekers are called to walk as well as how to overcome challenges along the way.

Pulses of the Divine Heart is an uplifting and enriching study that attests to the abiding nature of God's love and the unfailing goodness of Providence to the faithful man whose spirit is in tune with the divine.

Etching for the Heart is a timely, fascinating and insightful study that highlights the power of sacrificial love, good hope and the enlightenment of Christ to bring wholeness in life of the believer.

No Hurry to Horeb is a thoughtful discourse about how mankind can tune his inner awareness to rise above the lowliness of today's society and realize the fullness of life divinely appointed for those who truly aspire.

Echoes of the Golden thoughtfully and deeply explores the path that leads to spiritual transformation so that mankind can begin to see from a heavenly perspective to make the earthly experience better.

Books of Original Poems by Kalu Onwuka

Anthems in the Glorious Dawn is a rich collection of ninety-three original poems to nourish the soul, uplift the spirit and help rekindle a relationship with God. The underlying message of the power of sacrificial love strikes a resonant chord.

In Enchantment of Eternity is a superb collection of ninety-four original poems that touches the heart deeply through such topics as love, the treasures of life's high road as well as the vision and victory availed through strong faith.

Tones of the Stellar is a volume of eighty eight inspirational poems that speaks to the freedom of spirit and wholeness of life availed by enlightenment through Christ. The remarkable verses offer guidance about reconnecting with God.

A Splendid Awakening is a simple yet eloquent collection of ninety-two inspirational poems that highlights how man must let go of his mistake-laden past to realize a fulfilling and enduring future full of God's blessing.

 *The Melody of Light* is a selection from the author's body of work that represents the very best of faith-based poetry. Brimming with insights and thoughtful lessons, the verses paint vivid images about the wholeness that love avails.

All titles are available as paperbacks or e-books and may be purchased through many retail outlets and on-line distribution channels including **amazon.com**. All titles may also be purchased through Granada Publishers at **www.granadapublishing.com** and excerpts of the author's work are available at **www.kaluonwuka.com**.

Kalu Onwuka is a prolific author who writes about faith-walk and the path to transformation within for better in this new age of spiritual awareness. A vanguard among the emerging breed of spiritual poets, he uses his works to highlight the path that mankind must walk in order to find a blissful balance between the earthly and the heavenly.

He is the author of *Ruminations on the Golden Strand* series which are in-depth studies based on spiritual and earthly experiences that frame modern living in a way to help mankind achieve the utmost within a relationship with the Divine. The series include *Nuggets of Resurrection, Pulses of the Divine Heart, Etching for the Faithful Heart, No Hurry to Horeb,* and *Echoes of the Golden.*

He is also the author of *Poems in Faithfulness to the Divine* series which are books of poetry and songs. These include *Anthems in the Glorious Dawn, In Enchantment of Eternity, Tones of the Stellar, A Splendid Awakening* and *The Melody of Light.* There are other works on the way including the forthcoming *Capsules of Divine Splendor.*

Onwuka is a teacher, poet, lyricist, electrical engineer and entrepreneur. He lives in California with his wife of many years with whom he has raised five children. As a follower of Christ Jesus as the Light of the world, he believes that all true spiritual paths eventually converge in Christ. He uses his writing to help many achieve spiritual transformation for a more fulfilling life.

www.ingramcontent.com/pod-product-compliance
Lightning Source LLC
Chambersburg PA
CBHW060151050426
42446CB00013B/2769